the

RESTING
PLACE

DESTINY IMAGE BOOKS BY BILL JOHNSON

BILL
JOHNSON

the

RESTING
PLACE

LIVING IMMERSED IN THE
PRESENCE OF GOD

But the Helper, the Holy Spirit, whom the Father will send in My name, He will teach you all things, and bring to your remembrance all that I said to you.

(John 14:26 NASB)

NO GREATER PRIVILEGE

There is no greater privilege than being a host to God Himself. Neither is there a greater responsibility. Everything about Him is extreme. He is overwhelmingly good, awe-inspiring to the max, and frighteningly wonderful in every possible way. He is powerful yet gentle, both aggressive and subtle, and perfect, while embracing us in the midst of our imperfections. Yet few are aware of the assignment to *host Him*. Fewer yet have said yes.

The idea of hosting God may sound strange. He owns everything, including our own bodies. And He certainly doesn't need our permission to go somewhere or do anything. He is God. But He made the earth for humanity and put it under our charge.

If you were renting a home from me, I wouldn't walk into your home without an invitation, or at least without your permission. You would never see me in your kitchen, taking food from your refrigerator and cooking a meal for myself. Why? Even though it is my house, it is under your charge or stewardship. While there may be landlords who would violate such protocol, God is not one of them.

He planted us here with a purpose. Yet it's a purpose we can't accomplish without Him. Our true nature and personality will never come to fullness apart from His manifest Presence. Learning to host Him is at the center of our assignment...[1]

---

1   Hosting the Presence, p. 28

In Him also we have obtained an inheritance, having been predestined according to His purpose who works all things after the counsel of His will, to the end that we who were the first to hope in Christ would be to the praise of His glory. In Him, you also, after listening to the message of truth, the gospel of your salvation—having also believed, you were sealed in Him with the Holy Spirit of promise, who is given as a pledge of our inheritance, with a view to the redemption of God's own possession, to the praise of His glory.

(Ephesians 10-14 NASB)

UNCOVERING
THE DEPTHS

One of the Holy Spirit's primary functions is to discover what lies in the depths of God's heart for us. He leads us into an understanding by experience to help us realize our inheritance.

For to us God revealed them through the Spirit; for the Spirit searches all things, even the depths of God . . . Now we have received, not the spirit of the world, but the Spirit who is from God, so that we may know the things freely given to us by God, which things we also speak, not in words taught by human wisdom, but in those

*taught by the Spirit, combining spiritual
thoughts with spiritual words.*

(1 Corinthians 2:10, 12-13 NASB)

This inheritance is freely given to us; it is the
Holy Spirit who brings us into that *land of promise*
that we might correctly navigate our way through
life realizing the height, depth, length, and width
of God's extravagant love for us. He unveils what is
ours.[2]

Everything God created was made for His pleasure. He is a God of extravagant joy. He enjoys
everything He made. Humanity has a unique place
in His creation, though, in that we are the only part
of His creation actually made like God. Likeness
was made for the purpose of fellowship—intimate
communion. Through relationship with God, the
finite ones would be grafted into His eternal perfect

---

2   Dreaming with God, p.136

past and obtain through promise an eternal perfect future. Even the realm of impossibilities could be breached by those created to be like Him. *"All things are possible to him who believes"* (Mark 9:23). No other part of creation has been given access to that realm. We have been invited in a "place" known only by God.

The heart of God must be celebrated at this point: He longs for partnership. He risked everything to have that one treasure—those who would worship Him, not as robots, not merely out of command, but out of relationship.[3]

<hr />

3   Hosting the Presence, p. 43

INTO
ALL TRUTH

The Holy Spirit was given to prepare [the disciples] for revelation at a whole new level. He would take them where Jesus couldn't. Perhaps this is part of the reason Jesus said, *"It is to your advantage that I go . . ."* The indwelling Holy Spirit enables us to bear more of the revelation of Jesus than was possible for the original twelve disciples.

> *But when He, the Spirit of truth, comes, He will guide you into all the truth; for He will not speak on His own initiative, but whatever He hears, He will speak; and He will disclose to you what is to come. He will*

glorify Me, for He will take of Mine and will disclose it to you. All things that the Father has are Mine; therefore I said that He takes of Mine and will disclose it to you.

(John 16:13-15 NASB)

The Holy Spirit is assigned to take us into *all truth*. The word "all" here is staggering, and should be. What makes this even more stunning is the realization that truth is to be experienced; the Holy Spirit is therefore leading us into experiencing *all truth*. He receives all of His instructions from the Father. It was the Holy Spirit upon Jesus that enabled Him to know what the Father was doing and saying. That *same gift* of the Spirit has been given to us for that *same purpose*.

One of the assignments of the Holy Spirit is to let us know *what is to come*. If you read commentaries and various reference materials, you'll notice most think the promise of *knowing what's coming* is all about us being aware of coming calamities. Theologians tend to focus on problems because few truly believe in the glorious church. Everyone from world leaders to musicians, to actors and business leaders, are telling us of the coming calamities. We don't need the Holy Spirit for that purpose when people without God can do it. Rather, we need Him to see the coming glory! The warnings of difficulties are necessary as they help us keep our priorities straight. But it's the Father's good pleasure to give us the mysteries of the kingdom. And there's no pleasure in speaking of the death and destruction of the unrighteous. It's still called the *good news* for a reason.[4]

---

4   Dreaming with God, p. 135-136

THE GREATEST SEARCH ENGINE

Eye has not seen, nor ear heard, Nor have entered into the heart of man The things which God has prepared for those who love Him. But God has revealed them to us through His Spirit. For the Spirit searches all things, yes, the deep things of God.

(1 Corinthians 2:9-10)

The Holy Spirit searches for things that have never been heard by human ears or seen by human eyes. He is the greatest search engine in the whole universe. Talk about quick and accurate! He searches the greatest reservoir of information imaginable — the heart of the Father. Psalm 139:18 says God's thoughts about each one of us outnumber the sands on every seashore on this planet, and according to Jeremiah 29:11 all those thoughts are for your welfare, benefit and blessing. God has been around a long time, and He has had a long time to think about you. He's been living in the experience of knowing you long before you were ever born. He doesn't just have a few random thoughts about you here and there. For trillions of years, God has been thinking about you, and the Holy Spirit searches that whole archive and brings incredible treasures to you at precisely the right moment — if you're listening.[5]

---

5   Supernatural Power of the Transformed Mind, p. 60

IT'S IN THE BANK

I can die of starvation with a million dollars in the bank. If I don't make withdrawals from what's in my account, my wealth is no better than a dream, principle, or fantasy. Everything in our account in Christ is beyond our wildest dreams. We can't make a withdrawal if we don't know what exists.

Jesus models the mere beginning of what's in our account. The promises of His Word give us even greater insight to this superior reality. It's time to see what Jesus has, so we can see what Jesus gave us.

Here's the bottom line—He gave us everything that belongs to Him. And the Father gave Him everything! Look at it here in John 16:14–15, speaking of the work of the Holy Spirit— *"He will glorify*

Me, for He will take of what is Mine and declare it to you. All things that the Father has are Mine. Therefore I said that He will take of Mine and declare it to you." This really is an amazing passage of Scripture, one for which we bear great responsibility.

The Holy Spirit releases what Jesus alones possesses into our accounts through declaration. Every time He speaks to us, He transfers the eternal resources of Jesus to our account, enabling us to complete our assignment: *"Heal the sick, cleanse the lepers, raise the dead, cast out demons. Freely you have received, freely give—Go therefore and make disciples of all the nations, baptizing them in the name of the Father and of the Son and of the Holy Spirit, teaching them to observe all things that I have commanded you; and lo, I am with you always, even to the end of the age"* (Matt. 10:8; 28:19–20). Notice it says for the disciples to teach their converts all that Jesus taught them. That *must* include the instruction to heal the sick, cast out devils, etc. There was never to be a discrepancy between how we live today and His initial standard.[6]

---

6   God is Good, p.154-155

OUR GREATEST TREASURE

Our greatest treasure is God Himself. Our greatest privilege is to manifest Him. The people of God around the world are crying out for God to show up in a more significant way. It's a healthy cry. But tragically, history is filled with those who have praying that prayer for years without ever seeing a true visitation of God. Many of the highly respected books on revival were written by people who never took part in one.

Is it that hard to get God to show up? Jesus was born in a manger—He's not that picky. Such an absence of His manifested presence has been attributed to His sovereignty. But I think it's unfair to sweep unfulfilled promises into a category called *God's sovereignty*, where God gets blamed for any lack we experience by our just stating it was because of His mysterious ways.

The only time the disciples couldn't bring deliverance to a tormented child, they weren't content with the absence of a miracle, assuming it was God's sovereign will. And so, they asked Jesus. He demonstrated how and then told them why, and the child was set free. In other words, don't blame the Father. The lack is always on our end of the equation. The covenant is complete and effective for all.

God will allow us to carry as much of His presence as we're willing to jealously guard. It has never crossed our minds how much is available to us now. Moses, who was not even born again (because Jesus had not yet died for our sins), carried a measure of Jesus' presence that is unusual for today. That shouldn't be. Inferior covenants should not provide superior blessings. The blood of Jesus gives us access to a far greater glory than was ever experienced by Moses (see Cor. 3:7-11).[7]

7   Releasing the Spirit of Prophecy, p.174

MOSES,
A PROTOTYPE

*W*ould *that all the Lord's people were prophets, that the Lord would put His Spirit
upon them!*" (Num. 11:29). Moses was
a prototype in that he modeled a lifestyle that was
above the Law. Not in the sense that the Law didn't
apply to him. But he was above the Law in the sense
that he had access to the presence of God in a way that
was forbidden by the Law, even for the tribe of priests,
the Levites. As such, there's a part of Moses' lifestyle
that gives a prophetic picture of what would be possible under the new covenant that was yet to come.

As I look at Israel's journey, and the experiences with God from the many leaders in the

Old Testament, Exodus 33 is the Bible's standout chapter in my perspective. Moses had several face-to-face encounters with God. But only one time that he came down from his meeting with God on the mountain did his face shine with the Presence of God. He literally radiated God's Presence. Not until Jesus, on the Mount of Transfiguration, would we see that phenomenon again. (But with Jesus, even His clothes shone with God's glory.)

There was one significant difference in the outcome of this encounter with God. This is the time he asked to see the glory of God, and God let all His goodness pass before his eyes (Ex. 33:19). The outcome was that Moses' face shone because of seeing God's goodness. A revelation of God's goodness will change our countenance. God wants to change the face of His church once again through a revelation of His goodness. He longs to raise up a people who will not just carry good news in the form of words. He longs to raise up a people who carry the good news in power, which is a person (see 1 Cor. 4:20). It's Presence.[8]

---

8   Hosting the Presence, p.58

For by one Spirit we were all baptized into one body, whether Jews or Greeks, whether slaves or free, and we were all made to drink of one Spirit.

(1 Corinthians 12:13 NASB)

THE
ULTIMATE GOAL

There is a difference between immediate and ultimate goals. Success with an immediate goal makes it possible to reach an ultimate goal. But failure in the immediate prevents us from reaching our final goal.

Bowlers know this. Each lane not only has ten pins at the far end, it also has markers on the lane itself. A good bowler knows how his or her ball rotates as it is released from a hand. Bowlers will aim at a marker in the lane as an initial target. Yet they receive no points for hitting it. Points are only given when the ultimate target is hit—the pins at the end of the lane.

Likewise, salvation was not the ultimate goal of Christ's coming. It was the immediate target... the marker in the lane. Without accomplishing redemption, there was no hope for the ultimate goal—which was to fill each born again person with the Holy Spirit. God's desire is for the believer to overflow with Himself, that we might *be filled with all the fullness of God*" (Eph. 3:19). The resulting fullness of the Spirit was different than anyone had ever before experienced. For that reason, the greatest of all Old Testament prophets could confess: "I need to be baptized by you," meaning, "I need your baptism...the one I was assigned to announce!"

The baptism in the Holy Spirit makes a lifestyle available to us that not even John had access to. Consider this: we could travel off of this planet in any direction at the speed of light, 186,000 miles a second, for billions of years, and never begin to exhaust what we already know to exist. All of that rests in the palm of His hand. And it's *this* God who wants to fill us with His fullness. That ought to make a difference!

He'll give us His baptism of fire if we'll give Him something worth burning.

This baptism in the Holy Spirit is the fulfillment of the Old Testament picture of entering the Promised Land. Suppose the children of Israel had chosen to cross the Jordan but became content to live on the banks of the river. They would have missed the purpose for crossing the river in the first place. There were nations to destroy and cities to possess. Contentment short of God's purposes would mean having to learn to live with the enemy. That is what it is like when a believer is baptized in the Holy Spirit but never goes beyond speaking in tongues. When we become satisfied apart from God's ultimate purpose of dominion, we learn to tolerate the devil in some area of our life. As glorious as the gift of tongues is, it is an entrance point to a lifestyle of power. That power has been given to us that we might dispossess the strongholds of hell and take possession for the glory of God.[9]

---

9   When Heaven Invades Earth, p.79-80, 80-81

BAPTISM
OF FIRE

I have a Pentecostal background, for which I am very thankful. My forefathers paid quite a price to preach and defend that the baptism in the Spirit and speaking in tongues is still for today. I owe it to them to do nothing to take away from their accomplishments, but add all I can. Having said that, I have seen that many have come to the wrong conclusions about this Holy Spirit baptism. It's not for tongues (which I believe is important and available to *everyone*). It's for *power*. And it's not just power for miracles. It's so that the power-charged atmosphere of Heaven can rest upon a person, which forces a shift in the atmosphere over a home, business, or city. This baptism is to make us living witnesses and examples of the resurrection of Jesus—the ultimate display of Heaven's power. The Spirit of the resurrected Christ is what filled the air on the day of Pentecost.[10]

I can only imagine that after ten days of praying together [the disciples] were tired and had probably exhausted everything they could think of to pray about. Suddenly, their affection for Jesus was taken to a level they had never known or experienced before. Their spirits became empowered by the Holy Spirit in that *suddenly* moment. They were alive, really alive for the first time in their lives. They spoke of things they didn't understand. Two worlds collided. And the understanding of God that exists in that heavenly realm actually influenced the language of the one hundred and twenty here on earth. They spoke of the mysterious ways and the mighty deeds of God.

10   Hosting the Presence, p.106

This baptism is likened unto *wine* and not *water*. Water refreshes while wine influences. When God calls a particular baptism a *baptism of fire*, it is obviously not one of mere refreshing. Heaven has come to influence earth in this baptism.[11]

---

11 Hosting the Presence, p. 107

THE FATHER'S PROMISE

On the day of Pentecost, the baptism in the Holy Spirit was given. This baptism in the Holy Spirit is called the Father's Promise. The Father, the One who only gives good gifts, has given us this gift. All life flows only from Him. He is the One who is the orchestrator and conductor of life, and He has given a promise. And this is it. This is His special gift. It's a promise that reintroduces us to the original purpose for humanity: a people suited to carry the fullness of God on earth (Eph. 3:19). This is only possible through the baptism in the Holy Spirit—a baptism of fire!

And suddenly there came from heaven a noise like a violent rushing wind, and it filled the whole house where they were sitting

(Acts 2:4).

A noise came from Heaven. Two worlds met. It was like a violent rushing wind. The word *rushing* is *phero*. Out of the 67 times that word is translated in the New Testament, it is *rushing* only once. The other times it has the meaning *to carry*, *to bear*, or *to bring forth*.

It would be foolish for me to suggest changing how it's translated. But I would like to suggest adding the *bring forth* aspect to our understanding of its meaning. So then the word *rushing* could imply that this was a noise, a violent wind, that *carried* or *brought forth* something from its place of origin to its destiny: from Heaven to earth? I think so.

Noise can be translated *roar*. God spoke the worlds into being. His word is the creative force. *"By the word of the Lord the heavens were made, and by the breath of His mouth all their host"* (Psalm

I have filled him with the Spirit of God in wisdom, in understanding, in knowledge, and in all kinds of craftsmanship, to make artistic designs for work in gold, in silver, and in bronze, and in the cutting of stones for settings, and in the carving of wood, that he may work in all kinds of craftsmanship.

(Exodus 31:3-5 NASB)

Artistic design, *excellence*, and *inventive work* are a few of the characteristics of wisdom in this passage. That is part of what being filled with the Spirit looked like in Moses' day. The New Testament adds the power element, because every believer now has access to the miracle realm through the outpouring of the Holy Spirit. This new emphasis does not abolish the original revelation of the subject, but uses it as a foundation to build upon. If we combine the two we end up with believers who walk in wisdom, making practical contributions to the needs of society, who also confront the impossibilities of life through the provisions of the cross, bringing solutions through supernatural display of miracles, signs, and wonders. Perhaps it is these two things working in tandem that should be considered *the balanced Christian life.*[13]

---

13 Dreaming with God, p. 41-42

JOHN
THE BAPTIST

Jesus sets a standard with this statement—*John the Baptist was the greatest of all Old Testament Prophets*. He didn't do any miracles that we know of. His ministry was gloriously necessary, but not one we'd normally compare to some of the more spectacular prophets like Elijah or Daniel. Yet the One who knows all says he's the greatest. There is a truth contained in this passage that helps us to see our potential from heaven's perspective. It is such a wonderful truth that all of hell has made a priority of trying to keep us from its simplicity.

With that in mind, a more startling bit of news comes next—*He who is least in the kingdom of heaven is greater than he.* He wasn't saying that the people in heaven were greater than John. There's no purpose for such a statement. He was talking about a realm of living that was soon to become available to every believer. John prophesied of Christ's coming, and went so far as to confess his personal need of it.

> *He who is coming after me is mightier than I...He will baptize you with the Holy Spirit and fire.*
>
> (Matthew 3:11)

> *Jesus came to be baptized...John tried to prevent Him—"I need to be baptized by You..."*
>
> (Matthew 3:14)

John confessed his personal need of Jesus' baptism. Not one of the Old Testament prophets, not even John, had what was about to be offered to the *least of all saints*. It is the baptism in the Holy Spirit that became God's goal for mankind.

The baptism in the Holy Spirit makes a lifestyle available to us to which not even John had access. Jesus whetted our appetite for this lifestyle through His example, then He gave us the promise of its availability.[14]

14 When Heaven Invades Earth, p.78-79

A FLOWING
PRESENCE

Living a life filled with the Spirit of God is the only possible way I can consistently bring others into an encounter with God. Maintaining an awareness of Him, with the willingness to do whatever He wants, makes this challenging goal doable...

To illustrate what it looks like to be full of the Holy Spirit, I often take an unopened water bottle. I then ask the question, "Is this water bottle full?" And of course, the answer is yes. It is full by the acceptable standards set by the manufacturer. But it isn't really full, at least not as full as it could be. I then open the bottle and pour into it from another bottle until it overflows. Everybody seems to get the illustration quickly. It is only full when it is overflowing—fullness is measured in the overflow.

It's the same for us. Being filled with the Spirit does not point to an experience we might have had a certain number of years ago. It's not measured by what I contain, but by what flows from me. Only in the continual overflow of His presence through our lives are we truly full of the Holy Spirit. And it's in that condition that we are most likely able to bring others into an encounter with God.

The concept of His flowing from us might be a little abstract for some. But the idea has its roots in Jesus' teaching to His disciples. In John 7:38–39, Jesus said, *"He who believes in Me, as the Scripture said, 'From his innermost being will flow rivers of living water.' But this He spoke of the Spirit"*. The picture He gives us in this passage is profound. He is teaching us what happens when we minister in His anointing—what happens when God has His way through us. It's like a river flowing from us. And that river is the Holy Spirit.

It couldn't be clearer. He flows from us. And this time, the picture is not of a water bottle to contain Him. He is in us as a river to impact the spiritual geography around us. He lives in us, but He wants out—He is in us as a river, not a lake. He is a flowing presence, carrying the heart of the Father, desiring to saturate the land with the works of Jesus.[15]

---

15   God is Good, p. 206

DEPENDENT
ON MORE

Somehow I always thought that the baptism in the Holy Spirit was a one-time event; I received my prayer language and that was it. The Bible teaches differently. In Acts 2, we find 120 being baptized in the Spirit in the upper room. Yet, in Acts 4 we find some of the same crowd being *refilled*. Some have put it this way: one baptism, many fillings. Why? We leak.[16]

16 When Heaven Invades Earth, p.82

Many who speak in tongues think they are full of the Holy Spirit. Being full of Holy Spirit is not evidenced in tongues; it is evidenced by being full. How do you know when a glass is completely full? It runs over. Peter on the day of Pentecost is filled with Holy Spirit. In Acts 4, Peter joins many others in a prayer meeting. Their overwhelming expression was to cry out for more. Peter prayed for more. He did not pray for relief in the midst of persecution, but instead for more boldness, that expression that sometimes offends, so that he could go deeper into the realms of darkness and pull out more victims. And the Bible says, *"And when they had prayed, the place where they had gathered together was shaken, and they were all filled with the Holy Spirit and began to speak the word of God with boldness"* (Acts 4:31).

In Acts 2, Peter is filled. In Acts 4 he needs to be refilled. Why? If you are doing this right, you must get filled often. There is one baptism. But we are to live in such a way that we give away all we get, while our capacity for Him increases. When we live full of the Holy Spirit, experiencing overflow, only more of Him will do. Needing to be refilled is not a sign of something gone wrong. Continual dependence on *more* is a good thing.[17]

---

17 Hosting the Presence, p.109

BURNING
HEARTS

When Jesus appeared to two men on the road to Emmaus, He opened the Scriptures to explain why the Christ had to die. As yet they didn't know who He was, but they persuaded Him to stay for a meal. When He broke the bread, their eyes were opened, and then He vanished. Their response is one of my favorite ones in all of the Bible. *"Were not our hearts burning within us while He was speaking?"* (Luke 24:32). That is exactly what happens to me when I read of what this same Jesus has done in the lives of those who have given themselves for more. My hearts burns.[18]

---

18 Hosting the Presence, p.191

Charles Finney

Charles Finney is one of the great revivalists in American history...He writes of this unusual experience in his own autobiography.

He entered a factory one morning after breakfast. In a room filled with young ladies working on their weaving machines, looms, and spinning devices, two in particular stood out to him. They looked a bit agitated, but seemed to cover it with laughter. He said nothing, but walked closer, noticing that one was trembling so badly that she couldn't mend her thread. When he got to within about 8 to 10 feet they burst out in tears and slumped down. In moments nearly the whole roomful of workers was in tears. The owner, who was yet unconverted himself, recognized that this was a divine moment and ordered that his factory be shut down to give

his workers a chance to come to Christ. A mini-re-
vival broke out, which lasted several days. Nearly
the entire mill was converted during this time. It all
started with a man upon whom the Spirit of God
love to rest. And so without words a room full of
workers came under the conviction of the Holy
Spirit and a revival was born.[19]

---

19 Hosting the Presence, p.200-201

BURNING HEARTS, CONT'D.

William Seymour[20]

The Spirit began to fall in L.A., as people were radically filled and walked out into the streets speaking in tongues. Crowds began to grow at these home meetings, where Seymour was living with a host family. Before long, they were preaching from the front porch as people filled the streets to listen. Eventually, they moved into an old horse stable at 312 Azusa Street. It was in this stable in 1906 that the Pentecostal movement was officially born.

20 Crowder, 187-189.

People would fall over and weep. They would speak in tongues. They would laugh, jerk, dance and shout. They would wait on the Lord for hours, sometimes saying nothing. Seymour would often preach from his knees.

"No one could possibly record all the miracles that occurred there," writes charismatic historian Roberts Liardon. John G. Lake said of William Seymour that, "He had more of God in his life than any man I had ever met up to that time."

Prayer lasted all day and all night. Firemen were even dispatched to Azusa street, because people saw a "fire," which was actually just the visible glory of God resting on the exterior of the building. Similar occurrences have happened in a number of revivals, like the Indonesian revival, as recorded by Mel Tari in the 1970's, where firemen were also dispatched to a "glory fire" that was visible to everyone around.

Missionaries began coming to Azusa Street from around the world to catch the fire. People would fall over, get saved and begin speaking in tongues blocks away from the building, even though no one prayed for them, and they had no idea what was going on in the Azusa mission. Parishioners would also hit the streets, knocking on doors with little bottles of oil and asking to pray for the sick.

Seymour sought first and foremost to cultivate the presence of God in his meetings. If someone felt led, they would stand up and begin to pray or preach. If the anointing did not seem to be on a particular speaker, that person would sometimes get a gentle tap on the shoulder to hush up. Truly, the Spirit of God was the leader of those meetings.[21]

---

21 Hosting the Presence, p.196-197

BURNING HEARTS, CONT'D.

Dwight L. Moody[22]

It was some months later, while walking the streets of New York, that Dwight finally experienced the breakthrough for which he and Sarah Cooke had been praying together. It was shortly before his second and most important trip to England. R.A. Torrey had this to say about this significant advance in Moody's life:

Not long after, one day on his way to England, he was walking up Wall Street in New York; (Mr.

---

22 Roberts Lairdon, *God's Generals: The Revivalists* (New Kensington, PA: Whitaker House, 2008), 366-367.

Moody very seldom told this and I almost hesitate to tell it) and in the midst of the bustle and hurry of that city his prayer was answered; the power of God fell upon him as he walked up the street and he had to hurry off to the house of a friend and ask that he might have a room by himself, and in that room he stayed alone for hours; and the Holy Ghost came upon him, filling his soul with such joy that at last he had to ask God to withhold His hand, lest he die on the spot from very joy. He went out from that place with the power of the Holy Ghost upon him, and when he got to London, the power of God wrought through him mightily in North London, and hundreds were added to the churches; and that was what led to his being invited over to the wonderful campaign that followed in later years.

Dwight describes the experience in this way:

I was crying all the time that God would fill me with His spirit. Well, one day, in the city of New York – oh, what a day! – I cannot describe it, I seldom refer to it; it is almost too sacred an experience for to name. Paul had an experience of which he never spoke for fourteen years. I can only say that God revealed Himself to me, and I had such an experience of His love that I had to ask Him to stay His hand. I went to preaching again. *The sermons were not different; I did not present any new truths, and yet hundreds were converted.* I would not now be placed back where I was before that blessed experience if you should give me all the world – it would be as the small dust of the balance.[23]

---

23 Hosting the Presence, p.191-192

BURNING HEARTS, CONT'D.

John G. Lake[24]

One afternoon a brother minister called and invited me to accompany him to visit a lady who was sick. Arriving at the home we found the lady in a wheel chair. All her joints were set with inflammatory rheumatism. She had been in the condition for ten years. While my friend was conversing with her, preparing her to be prayed with, that she might be healed, I sat in a deep chair on the opposite side of a large room. My soul was

24 *The John G. Lake Sermons on Dominion Over Demons Disease and Death,* Edited by Gordon Lindsay (Olendale, California: The Bhurr Press: Farson and Sons, 1949), 5–9.

crying out to God in a yearning too deep for words, when suddenly it seemed to me that I had passed under a shower of warm tropical rain, which was not falling upon me but through me. My spirit and soul and body, under this influence, was soothed into such a deep still calm as I had never known. My brain, which had always been so active, became perfectly still. An awe of the presence of God settled over me. I knew it was God.

Some moments passed; I do not know how many. The Spirit said, "I have heard your prayers, I have seen your tears. You are now baptized in the Holy Spirit." Then currents of power began to rush through my being from the crown of my head to the soles of my feet. The shocks of power increased in rapidity and voltage. As these currents of power would pass through me, they seemed to come upon my head, rush through my body and through my feet into the floor. The power was so great that my body began to vibrate intensely so that I believe if I had not been sitting in such a deep low chair I might have fallen upon the floor.

At that moment I observed my friend was motioning me to come and join him in prayer for the woman who was sick. In his absorption he had not noticed that anything had taken place in me. I arose to go to him, but I found my body trembling so violently that I had difficulty in walking across the room, and especially in controlling the trembling of my hands and arms. I knew that it would not be wise to thus lay my hands upon the sick woman as I was likely to jar her. It occurred to me that all that was necessary was to touch the tips of my fingers on the top of the patient's head and then the vibrations would not jar her. This I did. At once the currents of holy power passed through my being, and I knew that it likewise passed through the one that was sick. She did not speak, but apparently was amazed at the effect in her body.

My friend who had been talking to her in his great earnestness had been kneeling as he talked to her. He arose saying, "Let us pray that the Lord will now heal you." As he did so he took her by the hand. At the instant their hands touched, a flash of dynamic power went through my person and through the sick woman, and as my friend held her hand the shock of power went through her hand into him. The rush of power into his person was so great that it caused him to fall on the floor. He looked up at me with joy and surprise, and springing to his feet said, "Praise the Lord, John, Jesus has baptized you in the Holy Ghost!"

Then he took the crippled hand that had been set for so many years. The clenched hands opened and the joints began to work, first the fingers, then the hand and the wrist, then the elbow and shoulder.

These were the outward manifestations. But Oh! Who could describe the thrills of joy inexpressible that were passing through my spirit? Who could comprehend the peace and presence of God that thrilled my soul? Even at this late date, ten years afterward, the awe of that hour rests upon my soul. My experience has truly been as Jesus said: "He shall be within you a well of water, springing up into everlasting life." That never-ceasing fountain has flowed through my spirit, soul and body day and night, bringing salvation and healing and the Baptism of the Spirit in the power of God to multitudes.[25]

---

25 Hosting the Presence, p.197-200

THE
COMFORTER

I t's difficult for most to follow the leading of the Holy Spirit because we are so limited in our experience with Him. Most know Him only as the One who convicts of sin or gives comfort when we're troubled. The bottom line is we are not accustomed to recognizing the Holy Spirit's actual presence.

We are acquainted with a small list of acceptable manifestations that sometimes happen when He shows up, such as tears, or perhaps a sense of peace when our favorite song is sung. But few recognize just Him alone. To make matters worse, many unknowingly reject Him because He either shows up in a way that they are unaccustomed to, or He failed to come as He has in the past. (Consider the arrogance of automatically rejecting everything that we don't understand, or have never recognized the Scriptures to say. It implies that if God hasn't done it or shown it to us first, He wouldn't possibly do it to someone else.)

While few would admit it, the attitude of the Church in recent days has been, "If I'm uncomfortable with something, it must not be from God." This attitude has given rise to many self-appointed watchdogs who poison the Church with their own fears. Hunger for God then gives way to fear of deception. What do I trust most, my ability to be deceived or His ability to keep me? And why do you think He gave us the Comforter? He knew His ways would make us uncomfortable first.[26]

---

26 When Heaven Invades Earth, p.92

The trumpeters and singers performed together in unison to praise and give thanks to the Lord. Accompanied by trumpets, cymbals, and other instruments, they raised their voices and praised the Lord with these words: "He is good! His faithful love endures forever!" At that moment a thick cloud filled the Temple of the Lord. The priests could not continue their service because of the cloud, for the glorious presence of the Lord filled the Temple of God.

(2 Chronicles 5:13-14 NLT)

THROW OUT
THE LIST

His world has been breaking into ours with regularity in salvations, healings, and deliverances. The manifestations of that invasion vary. They are quite fascinating, and too numerous to catalog. While some are difficult to understand at first glance, we know that God always works redemptively.

On many occasions laughter has filled a room, bringing healing to broken hearts. Gold dust sometimes covers people's faces, hands, or clothing during worship or ministry time. Oil sometimes appears on the hands of His people; and it especially happens among children. A wind has come into a room with no open windows, doors, vents, etc. At some locations, believers have seen an actual cloud of His presence appearing over the heads of worshiping people. We've also had the fragrance of heaven fill a room.

In my own experience the fragrance of heaven filled our car while Beni and I were worshiping on a short trip. It lasted for about 30 minutes, and was a smell that I could actually taste, similar to granules of sugar sprinkled on my tongue. I have seen the small gems that suddenly appeared in people's hands as they worshiped God. Since early in 1998 we have had feathers fall in our meetings. At first I thought birds were getting into our air conditioning ducts. But then they started falling in other rooms of the church not connected with the same ductwork. They now fall most anywhere we go—airports, homes, restaurants, offices, and the like.

I mention this phenomenon because it seems to offend many that fully embrace this move of God...It's easy once we've made some adjustments in our belief system about what God can and will do, to think that we have stretched far enough. "Our beliefs now encompass the move of God." Nothing could be further from the truth. Like the generations before us they are dangerously close to regulating God's work by a *new and revised list of acceptable manifestations*. No longer is it just tears during a special song or a time of repentance following a moving sermon. Our new list includes falling, shaking, laughter, etc.

The problem is—it is still a list. And God will violate it. He must. We must learn to recognize His move by recognizing His presence. Our lists are only good for revealing our present understanding or experience. While I don't seek to promote strange manifestations, or go after *novelty*, I do refuse to be embarrassed over what God is doing. The list that keeps us from certain types of errors also keeps us from certain types of victories.[27]

---

27 When Heaven Invades Earth, p.159

PRAYING
GOD'S HEART

Perhaps the greatest understatement of this book would be that the Presence of God is discovered in prayer. And while that is an obvious truth, many people learn to pray without the Presence, thinking their discipline is what God is looking for. Discipline has an important part in walking with Christ, for sure. But Christianity was never to be known for its disciplines; it was to be known by its passions.

Prayer is the ultimate expression of partnership with God. It is the adventure of discovering and praying His heart. So many spend their life praying to God, when they could be praying with God. This partnership, with its answers and breakthroughs, is supposed to be the source of our fullness of joy.

But you, beloved, building yourselves up on your most holy faith, praying in the Holy Spirit.

(Jude 20)

With all prayer and petition pray at all times in the Spirit.

(Ephesians 6:18)

One who speaks in a tongue edifies himself.

(1 Corinthians 14:4)

When we pray anointed prayers, we are praying the heart of God. His heart is being expressed through words, emotion, and decree. Finding the heart of God is a sure way of locking into His Presence. This privilege of co-laboring is a part of the assignment given for those who would give themselves to carry His Presence well.[28]

28 One of the best books on this aspect of prayer is my wife's book, *The Happy Intercessor*, from Destiny Image Publishing.

Praying in tongues brings us edification and personal strength. In that kind of praying the Presence of God washes over us to bring great refreshing. I think it's a bit sad when people emphasize that tongues is the least of the gifts, which seems to give them the right to ignore it while they pursue the greater gifts. If one of my children took the birthday or Christmas gift I gave them and refused to open it because they discerned it was one of lesser value than the others, they'd hear a sermon from me they'd not soon forget. Any gift from God is wonderful, glorious, and extremely necessary to live in His full intentions for us. This particular gift is brilliantly useful for living in the Presence continually.[29]

---

29 Hosting the Presence, p. 173-174

Jesus of Nazareth was anointed by God with the Holy Spirit and with great power. He did wonderful things for others and divinely healed all who were under the tyranny of the devil, for God had anointed him.

(Acts 10:38 TPT)

JESUS, OUR EXAMPLE

But from the beginning, it has been God who continually sets the stage to partner with imperfect people in a co-laboring relationship. When I see that He did what He did as a man following His Father, then I am compelled to do whatever I need to do to follow that example. I am no longer content to live as I am. I will still celebrate His goodness, but now it will be from the very "trenches" that Jesus lived in.

There are two conditions put upon me in Jesus' example. These qualifications are essential for me to emulate the life, presence, and power that Jesus made evident. First is the fact that Jesus had no sin. Without

Jesus, I was hopelessly lost in sin. But I am no longer without Him, and never will be again. That lost condition is no longer a factor, nor is it my identity. Now I am found in Christ, without sin, because His blood has made me clean. Because of such overwhelming mercy and grace, I have met the first qualification.

The second condition is that Jesus was entirely empowered by the Holy Spirit. As a man, He was powerless. But the Spirit of God came upon Him in His water baptism (see Luke 3:21-22). It was right after that experience we see Him walking in power (see Luke 4:1, 14). When Jesus wanted His disciples to live in the same power that He did, He had them wait in Jerusalem that they might receive what was promised—the same outpouring of the Holy Spirit He received, now to be released upon them all (see Acts 1:8;2:1-4).

Jesus' life was an illustration of what one man could do who had no sin and was entirely empowered by the Holy Spirit. Jesus, who was entirely God, modeled life with the limitations of a man.[30]

---

30 God is Good, p.169-170

RELIANT UPON
THE ANOINTING

To fulfill His mission, Jesus needed the Holy Spirit; and that mission, with all its objectives, was to finish the Father's work (see John 4:34). If the Son of God was that reliant upon the anointing, His behavior should clarify our need for the Holy Spirit's presence upon us to do what the Father has assigned...We must be clothed with the Holy Spirit for supernatural ministry. In the Old Testament, it was the anointing that qualified a priest for ministry (see Exodus 40:15). According to Jesus' example, New Testament ministry is the same—anointing brings supernatural results.

This anointing is what enabled Jesus to *do only what He saw His Father do*, and to *say only what He heard His Father say*. It was the Holy Spirit that revealed the Father to Jesus.

It would seem that with all the significance attached to the name "Jesus," anyone desiring to undermine His work of redemption might be referred to as "Anti-Jesus," not "Anti-Christ." Even religious cults recognize and value of Jesus the man. At the very least, cults consider Him to be a teacher or a prophet and possibly "a" son of God. This horrendous error provides us with an understanding of why *antichrist* was the name given to this spirit of opposition. The spirits of hell are at war against the anointing, for without the anointing mankind is no threat to their dominion.

Jesus' concern for mankind was applauded. His humility was revered, but it was the anointing that released the supernatural. And it was the supernatural invasion of God Himself that was rejected by the religious leaders. This anointing is actually the person of the Holy Spirit upon someone to equip them for supernatural endeavors. So revered is the Holy Spirit in the Godhead, that Jesus said, *"Anyone who speaks a word against the Son of Man, it will be forgiven him; but whoever speaks against the Holy Spirit, it will not be forgiven him, either in this age or in the age to come"* (Matthew 12:32).[31]

---

31 When Heaven Invades Earth, p. 88

REND THE
HEAVENS

When Jesus was baptized in water, Heaven took notice. Here is an interesting description of this divine moment.

Immediately coming up out of the water, He saw the heavens opening, and the Spirit like a dove descending upon Him; and a voice came out of the heavens: "You are My beloved Son, in You I am well-pleased."

(Mark 1:10, 11)

Jesus saw the *heavens opening*. What had been promised through the ages had started. But no one expected this: Heaven invading earth through the humility of a man—the Son of God, the Son of Man.

The word *opening* means to *cleave, split:* It is translated as *opening, split,* and *tears* one time each, *divided* and *tear* two times each, and *torn* four times. Interestingly, it is the same word used to describe both the veil in the temple being *torn,* and the rocks *splitting* open at Jesus' death, as Heaven and earth shook as a witness to the injustice of that moment—one so perfect dying for those who deserve death. "*And behold, the veil of the temple was torn in two from top to bottom; and the earth shook and the rocks were split*" (Matt. 27:51). In other words, the *heavens opening* at Jesus' baptism by John was not a simple parting of the clouds. It was a violent act, first represented by Isaiah's language when he prayed, "*rend the heavens and come down*" (Isaiah 64:1). An invitation had been made on behalf of humanity, and God answered in person.

Tearing the heavens was in itself an act of ultimate grace and glory, resulting in spiritual forces of darkness suffering serious consequences. The man,

Christ Jesus, is now clothed with Heaven, thoroughly equipped for all His earthly purposes. And His equipping was a prophetic foretaste of what would soon be made available to all.[32]

---

32 Hosting the Presence, p.95-96

AWARENESS

L iving with a continual awareness of Him has got to be a supreme goal for anyone who understands the privilege of hosting Him. He is the *Holy* Spirit, making holiness a huge part of the focus of our lives. Yet He is as good as He is holy....

Every believer is aware of God, but not always at a conscious level. Developing this awareness is one of the most important aspects of our life in Christ. He is called, "God with us." Knowing Him that way is essential to our development.[33]

---

33 Hosting the Presence, p.157

Every believer experiences God's Presence in some way, but we often remain ignorant. This is especially so in a culture that has emphasized cognitive strengths over spiritual and sensual (physical sense) capabilities. For example, our bodies were created with the ability to recognize God's Presence. The psalmist said even his flesh cried out for the living God (Psalm 84, NKJV). The writer of Hebrews taught that a sign of maturity was the ability to discern good and evil through our senses: *"But solid food is for the mature, who because of practice have their senses trained to discern good and evil"* (Hebrews 5:14).

Those who are trained to recognize counterfeit money never study counterfeit money, as the possibilities for making fake money are endless. They immerse themselves in being exposed to the right currency. Then the bad automatically stands out. It's the same with developing our senses to discern good and evil. Immersion in the discovery of God's Presence upon us (the Spirit given without measure) will cause anything contrary to stand out. Generally, my heart can tell when something is right or wrong. But I've had Him speak in a way that only my natural senses could pick up what He was saying or revealing. He does this intentionally to train us as good soldiers in His army to hear in all contexts in which He may be moving or speaking. This makes us capable of being "instant in season and out."[34]

---

34 Hosting the Presence, p.158-159

TWO BIRTHS, TWO GARDENS

The first person to touch Jesus in His natural birth was obviously Mary, the virgin. But who was the first to touch Him at His second birth—His resurrection from the dead? Mary Magdalene! She's the one who had seven demons cast out of her and was healed of infirmities (see Mark 16:9)! The Virgin Mary, representing purity and all that is right, welcomed Jesus into the world for His role of fulfilling the Law and becoming the perfect sacrifice.

Mary Magdalene, the one who had been sick and tormented by devils, represents the unanswerable needs of the spirit, soul, and body. She welcomed Him into the world for His role of building a family out of the least pure or qualified in any way. The Virgin introduced the One who would close out the dispensation of the Law. The tormented one introduced Jesus into the season of grace where everyone would be welcomed.

In the first Garden, the Presence was taken for granted. God walked in the Garden one more time after Adam and Eve ate of the forbidden fruit. Their eyes were opened to their condition and they covered themselves with fig leaves to hide their nakedness. Then they hid from God, Himself. It was the last time we hear of God walking in the Garden to be with man.

In this garden, Mary would make sure that that mistake would not be repeated. She grabbed the resurrected Christ and wouldn't let go, until Jesus informed her that He had not even ascended to the Father yet. Jesus' promise of sending the Holy Spirit would now have to take on very practical expression for this one who had to have more of God. She had found the one thing—the Presence of God.[35]

---

35 Hosting the Presence, p.47

SUPERNATURAL
INVASION

B y far the greatest gift ever received by us is
the Holy Spirit Himself. Those who discover
the value of His presence enter realms of intimacy with God never previously considered possible. Out of this vital relationship arises a ministry of
power that formerly was only a dream. The incom-
prehensible becomes possible because He is with us.

I will be with you is a promise made by God
to all His servants. Moses heard it when he faced
the challenge of delivering Israel from Egypt (see
Exodus 3:12). Joshua received this promise when
he led Israel into the Promised Land (see Joshua
1:9). When Gideon received the call of God to be

a deliverer for Israel, God sealed it with the same promise (see Judges 6:16). In the New Testament, this promise came to all believers through the Great Commission (see Matthew 28:19). It comes when God has required something of us that is humanly impossible. It's important to see this. It's the Presence of God that links us to the impossible. I tell our folks, *He is in me for my sake, but He's upon me for yours.* His presence makes anything possible!

God doesn't have to try to do supernatural things. He is supernatural. He would have to try to not be. If He is invited to a situation, we should expect nothing but supernatural invasion.[36]

---

36 When Heaven Invades Earth, p.83

MAKING
HISTORY

The release of a gift through the laying on of hands is entirely God's doing. We are not vending machines where you put in your request, push a button, and out comes the desired gift. Often someone will tell me that they want twice what I have. Well, so do I! If it were that easy, I would lay hands on myself and pray, "Double it!" Of late, I've been telling people, "I can lay hands on you and impart an anointing into your life as God wills. But I can't give you my history with God."

There is something priceless in a person's life that must be developed and protected at any cost: it's our private history with God. If you make history with God, God will make history through you. This history is created when no one is watching—it's who we are when we are alone. It's seen in the cry of our hearts, how we think, what we pray, and how we value God, Himself. Our lives are shaped when there is no one able to applaud our sacrifice or efforts.

These are the moments that we learn the most about hosting His Presence. It's when there's no one to pray for, no one to serve—that's where the relational boundaries are determined. Am I in this for how God can use me, or am I surrendered because He is God, and there is no greater honor in life? Jesus had His encounter with the Holy Spirit at His water baptism. A crowd watched. Probably very few, if any, had an idea of what was happening. But it was on the nights on the mountain, when no one was watching, that His greatest breakthroughs came. History was made in Him before history was made through Him. He loved the Father before He could reveal the Father.[37]

---

37 Hosting the Presence, p. 180-81

Moses said to the Lord, "See, you say to me, 'Bring up this people,' but you have not let me know whom you will send with me. Yet you have said, 'I know you by name, and you have also found favor in my sight.' Now therefore, if I have found favor in your sight, please show me now your ways, that I may know you in order to find favor in your sight. Consider too that this nation is your people." And he said, "My presence will go with you, and I will give you rest." And he said to him, "If your presence will not go with me, do not bring us up from here. For how shall it be known that I have found favor in your sight, I and your people? Is it not in your going with us, so that we are distinct, I and your people, from every other people on the face of the earth?"

(Exodus 33:12-16 ESV)

A NEW SEASON

John testified saying, "I have seen the Spirit descending as a dove out of heaven, and He remained upon Him. I did not recognize Him, but He who sent me to baptize in water said to me, 'He upon whom you see the Spirit descending and remaining upon Him, this is the One who baptizes in the Holy Spirit.' I myself have seen, and have testified that this is the Son of God"

(John 3:32-34).

Jesus sets the stage for a whole new season. The Old Testament prophets modeled this possibility amazingly, especially for their day. They showed the impact of the Presence of God upon a person for a specific task. But it was Jesus who revealed this as a lifestyle. The Holy Spirit remained upon Him.

Now I realize that we are not to live by feelings. Emotions are wonderful, but not reliable indicators of God's Presence and moving. But there is a feeling that goes beyond emotions, and quite frankly can work regardless of our emotional state. It is the mood of the Holy Spirit Himself that we can become so in tune with that we move as He moves.

We know that the Holy Spirit lives in us as born-again believers. The amazing promise that accompanies this reality is that He will never leave us. What a promise. What a comfort this is. But the sad reality is that the Holy Spirit doesn't rest *upon* every believer. He is in me for my sake, but He is upon me for yours. When the Holy Spirit rests upon a person without withdrawing, He has been made welcome in a most honorable way.

I often ask people what they would do if an actual dove landed on their shoulders. How would they walk around a room, or even go about their day if they didn't want the dove to fly away? The most common answer is *carefully*. It's a good answer. But it's not enough. It is this—*every step must be with the dove in mind*. This is what I believe to be the key to *the Spirit that remains*. He is the single greatest reference point, not only for direction and power in ministry, but actually for life itself. We've been chosen to carry the Presence of God. Amazing.[38]

---

38 Hosting the Presence, p.137

HE RESTS
ON US

O nly priests can carry His Presence. Period.

God will not ride on ox carts, even though the Philistines seemed to get away with it (see 1 Samuel 4-6). The Presence of God will not rest on anything we make. He rests on us. I believe that applies to organizations, buildings, etc. People will often look at institutions that have been created to facilitate great ministries. But no matter how great the organization, the by-laws, or the reputation, God doesn't rest upon those things. It's people. Yielded people have the privilege of carrying (hosting) God into life's situations.[39]

---

39 Hosting, p. 122 (Rests on people, not on things)

All of life gets reduced to one thing—how we steward the Presence of God. Stewarding the Presence of God, hosting the Presence, is the only way these impossible dreams can be accomplished.

The fulfillment of these dreams is actually the byproduct of hosting Him well. Jesus affirmed this principle for life when He taught, "*But seek first His kingdom and His righteousness, and all these things will be added to you*" (Matt. 6:33). The Kingdom of God is not something separate from His actual Presence. The Kingdom has a King. In reality, the Kingdom of God is within the Presence of the Spirit of God. "*For the kingdom of God is...in the Holy Spirit*" (Rom. 14:17). This command by Jesus is to prioritize our lives down to the *one thing* which is eventually evidenced by righteous living.[40]

---

40 Hosting, p.100-101 (Steward presence)

IN AWE OF
HIS PRESENCE

The disciples lived in awe of this One who called them to leave everything and follow. It was an easy choice. When He spoke, something came alive in them that they never knew existed. There was something in His voice that was worth living for—worth giving one's life for.

Every day with Jesus was filled with a constant barrage of things they could not understand; whether it was a demoniac falling at Jesus' feet in worship, or the overbearing, religious leaders becoming silent in His presence; it was all overwhelming. Their lives had taken on a meaning and purpose that made everything else disappointing at best. Oh, they had their personal issues, for sure, but they had been apprehended by God and now nothing else mattered.

The momentum of the lifestyle they experienced would be hard for us to comprehend. Every word, every action seemed to have eternal significance. It must have occurred to them that to serve in the courts of this King would be far better than living in their own palaces. They were experiencing firsthand what David felt when he lived with God's presence as his priority.[41]

---

41 Dreaming with God, p. 23-24

COMMITTED
TO THE
RELATIONSHIP

I remember as a young man hearing someone talk about being full of the Spirit. Having strong Pentecostal roots, I didn't consider this a new subject. But what I heard taught that day was new. The man of God simply spoke of two verses, neither of which referred to the baptism in the Spirit. It's not as much in my heart to make a doctrinal statement right now as it is to make a relational statement. These two verses are guidelines.

Do not grieve the Holy Spirit of God.

(Ephesians 4:30)

Do not quench the Spirit.

(1 Thessalonians 5:19).

This simple insight took my focus from the expressions of the Spirit (gifts, etc.) and shifted them to what the Holy Spirit actually felt because of me. And the more I walk with the Holy Spirit, the more my priorities shift to contribute to this relationship. This opens up new realms in walking with God that I had not considered.

To not grieve the Holy Spirit is a command focused on the issue of sin: in thought, attitude, or action. "Grieve" is a word that means to cause sorrow or distress. It describes the pain the heart of the Holy Spirit can feel because of something we would do or allow in our lives. It is character centered. This is a boundary that must have the attention of anyone who is interested in hosting His Presence more powerfully.

To not quench the Holy Spirit is a command that zeroes in on the co-laboring aspect of our relationship. The word "quench" means to stop the flow of.

The original language defines it as to extinguish, or put out. This word brilliantly uses two metaphors to illustrate this connection with God. "To stop the flow" could be illustrated by bending a garden hose in half until water no longer flows from it, while "extinguish" portrays the passion part of our walk with God. To lose passion for God always affects our ability to allow the Holy Spirit to flow from us to change circumstances around us. This verse is power centered.[42]

---

42 Hosting the Presence, p.138-139

YIELDED
MIND

Every thought and action in your life speaks of allegiance to God or to Satan. Both are empowered by your agreement. Renewing your mind means learning to recognize what comes from hell, and what comes from heaven, and agreeing with heaven. That is the only way you will complete your divine assignment. God designed your mind to be one of the most supernaturally powerful tools in the universe, but it needs to be sanctified and yielded to the Holy Spirit so you can carry out His designs, creative ideas, and plans in your everyday life.[43]

---

43 The Supernatural Power of a Transformed Mind, p. 37

A yielded imagination becomes a sanctified imagination; and it's the sanctified imagination that is positioned for visions and dreams. There is great paranoia over the use of the imagination in the church of the western world. As a result, unbelievers often lead the way in creative expression – through the arts and inventions. They have no bias against imagination. The imagination is like a canvas to a painter. If it's clean, the artist has much to work with. God would love to use our imagination to paint His impressions upon; He just looks for those who are yielded. However, those who are preoccupied with "not being worthy" are too self-centered to be trusted with much revelation. At some point it has to stop being about us long enough to utilize the benefits of being in Christ for the sake of those around us. Such a position gives us unlimited access to the mysteries of God that enable us to touch the needs of a dying world.[44]

---

44   Dreaming with God, p.67

INTENSE
FOCUS

P salm 37 is one of my favorite psalms...Verse 7 tells us to "*rest in the Lord and wait patiently for Him*." Resting is a beautiful picture of people that no longer feel the pressure to strive to prove themselves. They are comfortable in their own skin. (Before we're saved we performed to get an identity so we'd be accepted. After we're saved we find out we're accepted, and that's our identity, and from there comes our performance.)

Patiently has two meanings: "pain in childbirth" or "whirling in the air in dance." Both of these activities require incredible focus and strength. We are to wait on God with an unflinching resolve and focus, much like what Jacob had when he wrestled the angel. The same can be said of Elisha when he contended for Elijah's mantle.

There are seasons in life when being involved in many diverse activities is not only acceptable—it's good. But there are also seasons when it is deadly...

Intense focus restricts what you are willing and able to see. And while this approach will keep you from seeing many things, it will also open your eyes to see more of what you hunger for. Self-control is not the ability to say no to a thousand other voices. It's the ability to say yes to the one thing so completely that there's nothing left to give to the other options.

The Holy Spirit is our greatest gift, and must become our single focus. With that in mind, each of us has become the target of God for a specific encounter that redefines our purpose on planet earth. It's the baptism of fire. We were born to burn. And while the danger exists of turning our attention from the person to the experience, it's worth the risk. No amount of miracles, no amount of insight, no amount of personal success will ever satisfy the cry of the heart for this baptism. And while many would like to just get it over with, often times there is a deep process involved. For the 120, it was ten days of continuous prayer. For me it was an eight-month season where my prayers actually woke me up. I didn't wake up to pray. I woke up praying.

Such a singleness of focus is rewarded. I personally don't think that these encounters are supposed to be a one-time event. We must have frequent encounters with God that continuously recalibrate our hearts that we might be entrusted with more and more of God.

What a person values they will protect. God will give us the measure of His presence that we are willing to jealously guard.[45]

---

45 Hosting the Presence, p. 189-190

Sing to the Lord, all the earth; proclaim his salvation day after day. Declare his glory among the nations, his marvelous deeds among all peoples. For great is the Lord and most worthy of praise; he is to be feared above all gods. For all the gods of the nations are idols, but the Lord made the heavens. Splendor and majesty are before him; strength and joy are in his dwelling place. Ascribe to the Lord, all you families of nations, ascribe to the Lord glory and strength. Ascribe to the Lord the glory due his name; bring an offering and come before him. Worship the Lord in the splendor of his holiness. Tremble before him, all the earth! The world is firmly established; it cannot be moved. Let the heavens rejoice, let the earth be glad; let them say among the nations, "The Lord reigns!"

(1 Chronicles 16:23-31 NIV)

HOW TO SEE

G od is very committed to teaching us how to see. To make this possible He gave us the Holy Spirit as a tutor. The curriculum that He uses is quite varied. But the one class we all qualify for is the greatest of all Christian privileges— worship. Learning *how to see* is not the purpose for our worship, but it is a wonderful by-product.

Those who worship in spirit and truth, as mentioned in John 4:23-24, learn to follow the Holy Spirit's lead. His realm is called the kingdom of God. The throne of God, which becomes established upon the *praises of His people* (see Ps. 22:3), is the center of that Kingdom. It's in the environment of worship that we learn things that go way beyond what our intellect can grasp (see Eph. 3:20)—and the greatest of these lessons is the value of His Presence. David was so affected by this that all his other exploits pale in comparison to his abandoned heart for God. We know that he learned to see into God's realm because of statements like, *"I have set the Lord always before me; because He is at my right hand I shall not be moved"* (Ps. 16:8). The Presence of God affected his seeing. He would constantly practice recognizing the Presence of God. He saw God daily, not with the natural eyes, but with the eyes of faith. That priceless revelation was given to a worshiper.

The privilege of worship is a good beginning place for those unaccustomed to addressing some of these kinds of themes found in Scripture. It's in that wonderful ministry that we can learn to pay attention to this God-given gift: the ability to see with the heart. As we learn to worship with purity of heart, our eyes will continue to open. And we can expect to see what He wants us to see.[46]

---

46 When Heaven Invades Earth, p.46-47

RESPONSE
TO WORSHIP

King David would later discover some things about God's response to worship that were unknown in Moses' time. Each generation has access to more than the previous. It is God's law of compound interest. Specifically, David recognized how God responds to the praises of His people. God responds with His Presence—He comes. This call of God upon the nation of Israel was to leave Egypt in order to worship. They were becoming a people who would be known by the Presence of God. He would become the distinguishing factor.

God's heart was for His entire nation of Israel to become priests. In fact, He commanded Moses to tell Israel of His desire. *"And you shall be to Me a kingdom of priests and a holy nation"* (Ex. 19:6). Priests minister to God. The plan of God having a people of His Presence was well underway.

Worship is powerful for many reasons. One of the most important is that we always become like the One we worship. This by itself would take Israel to new levels. But this call of God upon the nation of God would not go unnoticed.

The devil is very afraid of a worshipping people. He actually doesn't mind complacent worship, as it seems to work opposite to the real thing—it deadens our sensitivities to the Holy Spirit of God. It works completely opposite to the effects of sold out, passionate worship. Complacent worship is an oxymoron.[47]

---

47 Hosting the Presence, p. 54-55

FROM SAUL
TO DAVID

When David became king, He wanted the Ark of the Covenant, the dwelling place of God among mankind, in his city of Jerusalem. So David pitched a tent on Mount Zion that housed the Ark of the Covenant.

Mount Zion is a small rise in the earth within the city of Jerusalem. That is where the presence of God rested for the benefit of the whole nation of Israel. We don't know the size of the tent. All we know is that God was there, and so were the priests. They ministered to God through thanksgiving, praise, and worship with their musical instruments, physical expressions like raising their hands, bowing low, the dance, as well as lifting up their voices.

The great honor for anyone, terrifying as it may have been, was to be able to come into the presence of the Almighty God. That very act was forbidden to them under the Law. But God in His mercy allowed them to taste of a New Testament reality long before its time. Under David, they did this daily. He had all the priests trained in music so they could lift up praises twenty-four hours a day, seven days a week. They took shifts so they could do this nonstop.

The priests had to shift their focus from the sacrifice of animals to the sacrifice of praise. Their role changed so dramatically that it would be hard for us to comprehend what it must have been like to serve under King Saul and then under David. The skills needed under one leader were completely useless under the next. They turned from the focus of keeping the Law to keeping the presence. An important feature to remember is that most of the time when the Bible talks about the presence of God, it's actually talking about His face. That is the meaning of the Hebrew word translated *presence*.

The prophet Amos declared that in the last days there would be a rebuilding of this tabernacle of David. The time of the fulfillment of this word would be when the Gentiles were added to what God was doing on the earth—they, too, would become His people. After the Great Commission given to the Church by Jesus to *"go into all the world"* (Matt. 28:19), followed by the outpouring of the Holy Spirit that would help them be effective (see Acts 2), Gentiles began to be added to the church. It became so controversial that the leaders of the church called a meeting in Jerusalem (see Acts 15). The conclusion of this gathering of apostolic leaders was that the inclusion of Gentiles to the faith was in fact from God. They were to be careful *not* to burden them with the requirements of the Law that they, themselves, could not keep. The Old Testament Scripture they used to support this idea was the Amos 9:11-12 passage:

"In that day I will raise up the fallen booth of David, and wall up its breaches; I will also raise up its ruins and rebuild it as in the days of old; that they may possess the remnant of Edom and all the nations who are called by My name," declares the Lord who does this.

Notice that the rebuilding of this tabernacle, known for the abiding presence of God and the worship from the priests, coincides with Gentiles being added to the faith. There is a connection in the unseen realm between the effect of worship and the conversion of souls.

The Tabernacle of David changed the focus of life and ministry for all priests in the Old Testament. It's a good thing, too. In the New Testament, we discover that every believer is now a priest unto the Lord (see 1 Peter 2:9). The Old Testament priesthood would be impossible for a New Testament believer to emulate, as it was focused on the sacrifice of animals and the worship of God in one location—the tabernacle or temple, depending on the time period. So this Old Testament story is once again a prophetic prototype of what we are to become.

We now have the privilege of ministering to God as they did in David's tabernacle. And the beautiful thing for us all is that this worship can and must be done in our homes, our cars, as well as in the corporate gatherings with our brothers and sisters. Such a role has such a dramatic effect on the atmosphere here on earth that people become converted. My thinking is that the atmosphere in our homes and churches becomes so saturated with the glory of God in response to our worship that people are able to see and hear truth clearly. Worship clears the airwaves. In that sense the Tabernacle of David, and its corresponding role in worship, is unchanged from the Old Testament to the New. Further study will again verify that the ministry of thanksgiving, praise, and worship—all aspects of our ministry unto Him—are all unchanged by the cross. In fact, it was the cross that brought this prototype out of the laboratory of an Old Testament experiment into the daily life of God's people, who have become His eternal dwelling place. It has become a norm.[48]

Psalms is the great book of worship. Songs were written to exalt God. But something unique happened in a few of these psalms. The writer would start to make declarations about the nations rising up to give God glory. Decrees were made about every nation worshipping the one true God. Now, regardless of where you think this fits into God's plan for the nations, worshippers first declare it. Why? Worshippers are in a place to call nations into their purpose, into their God-given destiny. It is the sacred privilege of those who worship.[49]

---

48 God is Good, p.79-82
49 Hosting the Presence, p. 128

SACRIFICE OF THANKSGIVING

Under the Old Covenant, the priest could only enter into God's Presence through a blood sacrifice. And then only the high priest could come into the Holy of Holies one day a year, the Day of Atonement. The Holy of Holies is the inner room where the manifest Presence of God was—the only light was the glorious Presence of God. This is where the Ark of the Covenant was kept.

When David became king, he sensed that God was looking for something else—priests that offer the sacrifices of thanksgiving and praise through a yielded and contrite heart. This was done even though the Law he lived under forbid it. It was offered with musical instruments as well as the voices of the singers. In this context, every priest could come daily before God without having to bring a blood offering. This order of worship was done twenty-four hours a day, seven days a week. This, of course, spoke of the day when every believer, a priest according to First Peter 2:9, would come to God in boldness because of what Jesus accomplished on our behalf. This is what was referred to when James said David's booth was being rebuilt.

David was the man after God's heart. He had a perception of God that would not be fully realized until Jesus would come and shed His blood for all. David's experience was a prophetic foretaste of something to come. I believe it was David's hunger for God that enabled him to pull this experience into his day, even though it was reserved for another day.[50]

---

50 Hosting the Presence, p. 126-127

EXTRAVAGANT
WORSHIP

It is worth noting that the ark of the covenant (the Presence of God) followed David into Jerusalem. Wherever David danced, God followed. He responds to our offerings. In this story, it's an offering of thanksgiving and praise expressed in the dance. Many respond to God once His Presence is realized. But some respond before He actually comes: they are the ones that usher in the Presence of the King of Glory. Another way of looking at it is God showed up wherever King David danced in an undignified fashion. It might surprise us to find out what is attractive to Him.

There was one notable absentee. Michal, the daughter of Saul, looked at the event through the palace window. Extreme worship always looks to be extreme foolishness to those who stand at a distance. Some things can only be understood from within. Such is the case with authentic worship.

Michal was appalled at David's lack of regard for how people perceived his passion, his humility in attire, and his complete lack of regard for public decorum. Instead of greeting him with honor, she tried to shame him when he returned home.

> But when David returned to bless his household, Michal the daughter of Saul came out to meet David and said, "How the king of Israel distinguished himself today! He uncovered himself today in the eyes of his servants' maids as one of the foolish ones shamelessly uncovers himself!"
>
> (2 Samuel 6:20)

His response was bold in many ways.

So David said to Michal, "It was before the Lord, who chose me above your father and above all his house, to appoint me ruler over the people of the Lord, over Israel; therefore I will celebrate before the Lord. I will be more lightly esteemed than this and will be humble in my own eyes, but with the maids of whom you have spoken, with them I will be distinguished."

(2 Samuel 6:21, 22)

David made it clear that God chose him above her father. This was a biting comment to say the least. Her disregard for the Presence of God revealed that she carried some of the same *lack of value* for the Presence that her father Saul had lived by during his reign. Never should we dumb down our emphasis on the Presence to accommodate the Michals in the house. He followed that comment by stating that she basically hadn't seen anything yet. In other words, if that embarrassed her, her future was not too bright. David was just getting warmed up. Tragically, *"Michal the daughter of Saul had no child to the day of her death"* (2 Sam 6:23).

Whenever someone despises extravagant worship, they put themselves in an extremely dangerous position. Barrenness is the natural result of despising worship. In doing so they are rejecting the reason we are alive. Barrenness and the absence of worship go hand in hand.[51]

---

51 Hosting the Presence, p. 123-125

It is the Spirit who gives life; the flesh profits nothing. The words that I speak to you are spirit, and they are life.

(John 6:63 NKJV)

All Scripture is given by inspiration of God, and is profitable for doctrine, for reproof, for correction, for instruction in righteousness, that the man of God may be complete, thoroughly equipped for every good work.

(2 Timothy 3:16-17 NKJV)

DEPENDENT ON
THE HOLY SPIRIT

To value the scriptures above the Holy Spirit is idolatry. It is not Father, Son, and Holy Bible; it's the Holy Spirit. The Bible reveals God, but is itself not God. It does not contain Him. God is bigger than His book.

We are reliant on the Holy Spirit to reveal what is contained on the pages of scripture because without Him, it is a closed book. Such dependency on the Holy Spirit must be more than a token prayer asking for guidance before a Bible study. It is a relationship with the third person of the Trinity that is continuous, ongoing, and affects every single aspect of life. He is the wind that blows in uncertain directions, from unknown places (see John 3:8). He is the power of Heaven, and cannot be controlled, but must be yielded to. He eagerly reveals His mysteries to all who are hungry – truly hungry. He is so valued in Heaven that He comes with a warning. The Father and Son can be sinned against, but sinning against the Holy Spirit has unforgivable eternal consequences.

The Holy Spirit is de-emphasized and almost removed from many Christian's daily approach to life and the Word. The fear of becoming like some mindless fanatic has kept many a Christian from interacting with their greatest treasure in this life – the Holy Spirit. We are heirs of God, and the Holy Spirit is the down payment of our inheritance (see Eph. 1:13-14). Some teach that we shouldn't talk much about the Spirit as the Holy Spirit doesn't speak of Himself. However, both the Father and Son have a lot to say about Him. It is wise to listen to them. God is to be praised, adored, boasted in, and interacted with – and the Holy Spirit is God.[52]

---

52 Dreaming with God, p.142

SACRED WRITINGS

The approach of many believers to Scripture is inconsistent with the Spirit who inspired those sacred writings. Much of what we have a heart to accomplish cannot be done without re-examining our relationship with God through His Word. We have gone as far as we can go with what we presently know. Not only are we in need of the Spirit of God to teach us, we are in need of a different view of the Bible.

The God who speaks through circumstances and unusual coincidences wants to talk to us again through the pages of His Word, even when it appears to be taken out of context or is not exactly in line with what appears to be the author's original intent.

The Word of God is living and active. It contains divine energy, always moving and accomplishing His purposes. It is the surgeon's knife that cuts in order to heal. It is balm that brings comfort and healing. But the point I wish to stress is that it is multidimensional and unfolding in nature. For example, when Isaiah spoke a word, it applied to the people he spoke to – his contemporaries. Yet because it is alive, much of what he said then has its ultimate fulfillment in another day and time. Living words do that.

God said we were to choose whom we would serve, yet Jesus said He chose us; we didn't choose Him. We are predestined from before the foundation of the world, yet are told that *whosoever will* may come. Jesus said we had to sell all to follow Him, yet He instructs the wealthy to be rich in good works. The Holy Spirit knows what truth to breath on according to the particular season of our life.[53]

---

53 Dreaming with God, p. 142-143

Truth is multidimensional. Some truths are superior to others. Lesser truths are often the foundation of greater truths. "*I no longer call you servants, but friends.*" Friendship with God is built on the foundation of first being a servant. Truth is progressive in nature – line upon line, precept on precept.

For example, the primary message of the Old Testament is to reveal the power of sin. For that reason when a person touched a leper, they became unclean. Sin is overpowering. Flee from it! The primary message of the New Testament is the power of God's love. So when Jesus touched a leper, the leper became clean. "*Love covers a multitude of sin.*" Both messages are true. One is greater.[54]

---

54 Dreaming with God, p. 144

WHEN
THE IMPOSSIBLE
BECOMES LOGICAL

Revelation that doesn't lead to a divine encounter will only make us more religious, teaching us to embrace external standards without the internal realities.

God is not opposed to the mind; He created the mind to be a compliment to all that He had made. He is opposed to the un-renewed mind. It is at war with God, being incapable of obeying Him (see Rom. 8:7). The believer who governs his Christian life through the mind is the carnal Christian that the apostle Paul warned about (see 1 Cor. 2-3). The soul can only lead us into religion – form without power. It is what makes way for Ishmaels instead of Isaacs.

It's important to understand the learning process. Our spirit is where the Holy Spirit dwells. Our spirit man is alive and well and is ready to receive great things from God. When I filter everything through my mind and remove what isn't immediately logical, I extract much of what I really need. Only what goes beyond my understanding is positioned to renew my mind (see Phil. 4:7).

If we can learn more about the actual voice and presence of the Lord, we will stop being so paranoid about being deceived by the things we can't explain. Usually those who use the natural mind to protect themselves from deception are the most deceived. They've relied on their own finite logic and reason to keep them safe, which is in itself a deception. They usually have an explanation for all that's going on in their walk with the Lord, but criticize those who long for more.

Our hearts can embrace things that our heads can't. Our hearts will lead us where our logic would never dare to go. No one ever attributes the traits of courage and valor to the intellect or the strength of human reasoning. Courage rises up from within and gives influence over the mind. In the same way, true faith affects the mind. Faith does not come from our understanding. It comes from the heart. We do not believe because we understand; we understand because we believe (see Heb. 11:6). We'll know when our mind is truly renewed, because the impossible will look logical.[55]

---

55 Dreaming with God, p. 58-59

REVELATION
TO SEE

The Holy Spirit lives in my spirit. That is the *place* of communion with God. As we learn to receive from our spirits we learn how to be Spirit led.

"*By faith, we understand*" (Heb. 11:3). Faith is the foundation for all true intellectualism. When we *learn to learn* that way, we open ourselves up to grow in true faith because faith does not require understanding to function.

I'm sure that most of you have had this experience—you've been reading the Bible, and a verse *jumps out at you*. There is great excitement over this verse that seems to give so much life and encouragement to you. Yet initially you couldn't teach or explain that verse if your life depended on it. What happened is this: Your spirit received the life-giving power of the word from the Holy Spirit. When we learn to receive from our spirit, our mind becomes the student and is therefore subject to the Holy Spirit. Through the process of revelation and experience our mind eventually obtains understanding. That is biblical learning—the spirit giving influence to the mind.[56]

Knowledge in this context is experiential knowledge. It is more than mere concepts or theories. The word *knowledge* here comes from the word used in Genesis describing the experience of intimacy – "*And Adam knew Eve; and she conceived and bare Cain*" (Gen. 4:1 KJV).

---

56 When Heaven Invades Earth, p.50

It is foolish to think, "Because we have the Bible, the full revelation of God has already been given. We don't need anymore." First of all, while the Bible is complete (no more books are to be added) it is a closed book without the help of the Holy Spirit. We must have revelation to see what is already written. Secondly, we know so little of what God wants us to understand from His Word. Jesus said as much. He couldn't teach His disciples all that was in His heart (see John 16:12). This is the knowledge that comes from the Spirit of God as He breathes upon the pages of Scripture. It leads to divine encounters; truth experienced is never forgotten.[57]

---

57 Dreaming with God, p. 128

KNOWN BY
PASSIONS

Doctrine must be a wineskin kept elastic by the oil of the Spirit. If it is rigid and unmoving, it will not yield to God's habit of opening up more of His Word to us. God loves to add to our knowledge things we think we already understand. Too much rigidity bursts our doctrinal wineskins under the weight of ongoing revelation. The end result is the church becomes irrelevant and powerless to the world around them....

The Holy Spirit has to be free to speak to us about the things that are on His heart; especially to those things we have natural resistance. We must be open to truth when it has a biblical basis and is accompanied by the breath of God making it come alive for a specific purpose. The error is building a theological monument around a particular point of view that conveniently excludes certain portions of scripture to help us feel secure in a doctrinal bent.

I am also concerned with our tendency to gather around doctrines instead of around spiritual fathers. The former builds denominations, while the latter creates movements. Even our most valued doctrines can be expanded under the inspiration of the Holy Spirit. Usually, it's not the expansion that we have the most difficulty with. It is when He begins to speak about what is, at first glance, a contradiction to what we have learned. The desire for rigid doctrine is in direct proportion to our inability to actually hear His voice. It's essential to be able to recognize His voice so we can embrace His revelation, even when it contradicts our traditional upbringing.

God is big enough to feed me from a particular verse every day for the rest of my life. The Word of God is infinitely deep. I must come to that which I understand with a childlike heart because what I know can keep me from what I need to know if I don't remain a novice. Becoming an expert in any area of scripture is the very thing that often closes us off from learning the new things that God is opening up in His Word. Again, it's the childlike heart that attracts revelation from God (see Matt. 11:25).[58]

The answer for many has been to take a more analytical approach to the Christian life, one that is stable in doctrine and disciplines but lives without personal experience, denies the opportunity for risk, and resists emotional expression and passion. Christianity was never to be known by its disciplines. It's to be known by its passion; and those without passion are in far more danger than they know. Demons are attracted to religiously sanitized environments where there is no power.[59]

---

58 Dreaming with God, p. 146-147

59 Dreaming with God, p. 151

FOLLOW THE LEADER

History provides us with a lesson from a great military leader. Alexander the Great led his armies in victory after victory, and his desire for ever greater conquest finally brought him to the foot of the Himalayas. He wanted to go beyond these intimidating mountains. Yet, no one knew what was on the other side. Senior officers were troubled by his new vision. Why? They had gone to the edge of their map—there was no map for the new territory that Alexander wanted to possess. These officers had a decision to make: would they be willing to follow their leader off the map, or would they be content to live within its boundaries? They chose to follow Alexander.

Following the leading of the Holy Spirit can present us with the same dilemma. While he never contradicts His Word, He is very comfortable contradicting our understanding of it. Those who feel safe because of their intellectual grasp of Scriptures enjoy a false sense of security. None of us has a full grasp of Scripture, but we all have the Holy Spirit. He is our common denominator who will always lead us into truth. But to follow Him, we must be willing to follow off the map—to go beyond what we know. To do so successfully we must recognize His presence above all.

There is a great difference between the way Jesus did ministry and the way it typically is done today. He was completely dependent on what the Father was doing and saying. He illustrated this lifestyle after His Holy Spirit baptism. He followed the Holy Spirit's leading, even when it seemed unreasonable, which it often did.

The Church has all too often lived according to an intellectual approach to the Scriptures, void of the Holy Spirit's influence. We have programs and institutions that in no way require the Spirit of God to survive. In fact, much of what we call ministry has no safeguard in it to ensure that He is even present. When our focus is not the presence of God, we end up doing the best we can for God. Our intentions may be noble, but they are powerless in effect.[60]

---

60 When Heaven Invades Earth, p. 85-86

WORD
OF GOD

While worship is the number one way that God has used to teach me about His Presence, a very close second would be my encounters with Him through His Word. I love the Scriptures so much. Most of what I have learned about the voice of God has been learned in the reading of His Word...

"So faith comes from hearing, and hearing by the word of Christ" (Romans 10:17). There are two important things I want to point to in this great verse. First is the fact that faith comes from hearing, not from having heard. The second is that faith doesn't necessarily come from hearing the Word.

Faith comes from hearing. Our capacity to hear comes from the Word. Being one who hears now is one who is in line for great faith. Our entire life is attached to His voice. Man lives by *"every word that proceeds out of the mouth of God"* (Matt. 4:4).[61]

---

61   Hosting the Presence, p. 178

O God, You are my God; I shall seek You earnestly; My soul thirsts for You, my flesh yearns for You, In a dry and weary land where there is no water.

(Psalm 63:1 NASB)

The Spirit and the bride say, "Come." And let the one who hears say, "Come." And let the one who is thirsty come; let the one who wishes take the water of life without cost.

(Revelation 22:17 NASB)

FORWARD
MOTION

Jesus was the fulfillment of an ongoing revelation of the heart of the Father. This revelation only increases from season to season. It's the principle given to us from Isaiah 9:7: *"There will be no end to the increase of His government or of peace."*

It only increases—goes forward. The concept of ongoing forward motion is repeated in 2 Cor. 3:18: *"from glory to glory."* The point is, God takes us forward in an ever-increasing revelation. It never declines or goes back to inferior standards, especially those of the Old Testament.

Once the demands of the Old were met (in and by Jesus), the New came into prominence, permanently. Once the real has become manifest (i.e., Jesus, the Lamb of God), we never go back to the symbolic (sacrificing sheep.) Once the Kingdom has become manifest, there's no going back.

If Jesus opened up the revelation of the Father through miracles, signs, and wonders, why would He then return to the inferior? He didn't. We did. And that's the point. To make sure we'd never forget the standard He set, He stated the impossible. *"Most assuredly, I say to you, he who believes in Me, the works that I do he will do also; and greater works than these he will do, because I go to My Father"* (John 14:12). Forward motion—that's the plan of God. No retreat. And, no excuses.[62]

---

62 God is Good, p. 153

BLESSED ARE THE POOR IN SPIRIT

In Matthew chapter 4, Jesus first declared the repentance message. People came from all over, bringing the sick and diseased, the tormented and handicapped. Jesus healed them all.

After the miracles He gave the most famous sermon of all time: the Sermon on the Mount. It is important to remember that this group of people just saw Jesus heal all kinds of sicknesses and perform mighty deliverances. Is it possible that instead of giving commands on the new way of thinking Jesus was actually identifying for them the transformation of heart they had just experienced?

"Blessed are the poor in spirit, for theirs is the kingdom of heaven" (Matt. 5:3). How would you describe a people who left cities for days at a time, traveling great distances on foot, abandoning all that life involves, only to follow Jesus to some desolate place. And there He would do what they had thought impossible. The hunger of their hearts pulled a reality from the heart of God that they didn't even know existed. Can their condition be found in the Beatitudes? I think so. I call them "poor in spirit." And Jesus gave them the promised manifestation of the Kingdom with healing and deliverance. He then followed the miracles with the Sermon, for it was common for Jesus to teach so He could explain what He had just done.

In this case, the actual presence of the Spirit of God upon Jesus stirred up a hunger for God in the people. That hunger brought a change in their attitudes without their being told it should change. Their hunger for God, even before they could recognize it as such, had created a new perspective in them that even they were unaccustomed to. Without an effort to change, they had changed.

How? The Kingdom comes in the presence of the Spirit of God. It was His presence they detected, and it was His presence they longed for. For them it didn't matter if He was doing miracles or just giving another sermon, they just had to be where He was. Hunger humbles. Hunger for God brings about the ultimate humility. And He *exalted them at the proper time* (see I Pet. 5:6) with a taste of His dominion.[63]

---

63 When Heaven Invades Earth, p. 40-41

KINGDOM
IN VIEW

"Repent, for the Kingdom of heaven is at hand" (Matt. 4:17). This word, *repent*, means "to change our way of thinking." But it is much more than a mental exercise. It really is the deep sorrow for sin that enables a person to truly repent and change his mind or perspective on reality. Hebrews 6:1 clearly teaches that there are two sides to this action: "*Repentance from dead works...faith toward God.*" Full repentance is *from* something *toward* something—*from* sin *toward* God. Many Christians repent enough to be forgiven but not enough to see the Kingdom. Their repentance doesn't bring the Kingdom into view.

The same concept is taught with two different perspectives. One passage (Hebrews 6:1) says *"toward God"* and the other (Matt. 4:17) implies it's *"toward the Kingdom."* Luke captures the richness of both views when he writes: *"Repent therefore and be converted, that your sins may be blotted out, so that times of refreshing may come from the presence of the Lord"* (Acts 3:19). The point is *the presence is the Kingdom.* It really is that simple.

It's too easy to complicate the Christian life. For example, we are told to put on the full armor of God, which includes the helmet of salvation, breastplate of righteousness, and so on (see Ephesians 6:10–18). The apostle Paul gave us this important instruction, but most of the time we miss the point. God *is* my armor. He's not saying, "Put something on that is a reality that is separate from Me." He's saying, "I'm it. Just abide in Me. I become your salvation. I am your righteousness, the breastplate over you. I am the Gospel of peace. I am the good news. I am the sword of the Spirit." This list paints a profound word picture enabling us to realize the fuller benefit of abiding in Christ. Simple is better.

Jesus tells us to repent because He brought His world with Him. If I don't shift my perspective on reality, I will never discover the superior reality—the unseen realm of His dominion. This kind of repentance enables a believer to live in *"heavenly places in Christ"* (see Ephesians 1:3). Discovering the presence of God is discovering the Kingdom.[64]

---

64 God is Good, p.72

RESTORED IN
HIS PRESENCE

Trust is the natural expression of the one in deep repentance. The nature of these two realities is portrayed well in Hebrews 6:1, *"repentance from dead works and of faith toward God."* In this one verse we see the nature of both repentance and faith—from and toward. The picture would be of one making an about face, from something and toward something. Here it is from sin toward God Himself. His Presence is discovered in repentance.

Repentance means to change the way we think. Our perspective changes regarding sin and God. With deep sorrow we confess (fully own up to our sin without excuse) and turn to God (upon whom we place our entire trust).

Similar imagery is given in Acts 3. "Therefore repent and return, so that your sins may be wiped away, in order that times of refreshing may come from the presence of the Lord" (Acts 3:19).

Note the end result—that times of refreshing may come from the presence of the Lord. In these two verses we see the pattern, the order that God created to lead us to Himself, to His manifest Presence. While we were sinners, God chose us to experience Him in such a way that we were fully restored to our original design, to live in and carry His Presence.

We are either walking in repentance, or we need to repent. Repentance is the lifestyle of being face-to-face with God. If that is missing, I must turn back. I must repent.[65]

---

65 Hosting the Presence, p. 173

LET ME KNOW
YOUR WAYS

We do well to pursue according to His commands. But romance is no longer romance when it is commanded. Some things must be pursued only because they are there. Moses was able to distill the cry of his heart in this simple prayer: *"Let me know Your ways that I may know You"* (Ex. 33:13). Discovering His ways is the invitation to come to Him and know Him in the way revealed. Revelations of His nature are invitations to experience Him. As He reveals His nature to us through the moving of the Holy Spirit, He will often leave us without command. Instead, He longs to discover what is actually in our hearts, as it is in the nature of the heart in love to always respond to the open door for encounter.[66]

It's not how extreme an encounter is with God. It's how much of us He apprehends in the experience—and how much of His presence He can entrust to us. Jesus manifested a lifestyle, as a man, that is intensely practical, and can no longer be avoided or considered unattainable. It is possible to carry the Presence of the Holy Spirit so well that the Father is revealed to this orphaned planet. That satisfies the quest for divine purpose quite well. Doing exactly as He did is what Jesus had in mind when He commission us in John 20:21.[67]

---

66   Hosting the Presence, p. 146
67   Hosting the Presence, p. 188

POWER COMES WITH ENCOUNTER

J ust as authority comes in the commission, so power comes in the encounter. We see it in Jesus' life, and so it is for the disciples. And it's no different for us. There is nothing that training, study, or association with the right people can do to make up for this one thing. There is nothing to replace a divine encounter. Everyone must have their own.

Tragically, many stop short of a divine encounter because they're satisfied with good theology. Once a concept is seen in Scripture, it can be shared with others even though there's no personal experience to back it up. True learning comes in the experience, not the concept by itself. Often we can become guilty of looking for something to happen to us that is on our list of what constitutes a "biblical" encounter with God. The lists of various experiences discovered in Scripture do not contain God; they reveal Him. In other words, He is bigger than His book, and is not limited to doing something for us the exact same way He did for someone else. He continues to be creative, each time revealing the wonder of who He is.

Many fail to realize that what is needed in this pursuit of more is an abandonment to God that attracts something that cannot be explained, controlled, or understood. We must encounter one who is bigger than we are in every possible way until He leaves a mark. It is wonderful, glorious, and scary.[68]

---

68 Hosting the Presence, p. 185

RELEASING
DOMINION

A reformation has begun. And at the heart of this great move of the Spirit is the total transformation of the people of God as they discover their true identity and purpose. Great purpose elicits great sacrifice. Up until this time, many of our agendas have failed. Our attempts to make the gospel palatable have had a serious effect on the world around us.

The world has longed for a message they could *experience*. Yet many believers have simply tried to make the good news more intellectually appealing. This must stop! The natural mind *cannot* receive the things of the Spirit of God (see 1 Cor. 2:14).

The wisdom of God is foolishness to men. It's time to be willing to appear foolish again, that we might provide the world with a message of power that delivers, transforms, and heals. This is true wisdom. It alone satisfies the cry of the human heart.[69]

But if I cast out demons by the Spirit of God, surely the kingdom has come upon you.

(Matthew 12:28)

Look at this phrase, "by the Spirit of God... the kingdom." The Holy Spirit encompasses the Kingdom. While they are not the same, they are inseparable. The Holy Spirit enforces the lordship of Jesus, marking His territory with liberty (see 2 Cor. 3:17). The *King's domain* becomes evident through His work.

---

69 Dreaming with God, p.49

The second part of this verse reveals the nature of ministry. Anointed ministry causes the collision of two worlds—the world of darkness with the world of light. This passage shows the nature of deliverance. When the Kingdom of God comes upon someone, powers of darkness are forced to leave.

When a light is turned on, darkness doesn't resist. There is no debate. It doesn't stay dark for a few minutes until light finally wins. On the contrary, light is so superior to darkness that its triumph is immediate.

The Holy Spirit has no battle wounds. He bears no teeth marks from the demonic realm fighting for preeminence. Jesus is Lord, period. Those who learn how to work with the Holy Spirit actually cause the reality of His world (His dominion) to collide with the powers of darkness that have influence over a person or situation. The greater the manifestation of His Presence, the quicker the victory.[70]

---

70 When Heaven Invades Earth, p. 82-83

AWARENESS
OF
HEAVEN

We cannot let darkness shape our awareness of the heavenly atmosphere that
dwells upon us. The *size* of the open
heaven over us is affected in some measure by our
maturity and yielded-ness to the Holy Spirit. Think
of the open Heaven as a big oak tree. The bigger and
more stable the tree is, the more people can stand
under its shade. Mature believers carry Heaven's
atmosphere in such a way that others are able to
stand under their shade and receive protection. To
use another analogy, others can *draft* on our breakthroughs and become changed.

To live unaware of the open Heaven over us is to contribute to the war over our hearts and minds as it pertains to the truth of Scripture. Then we will always see what hasn't happened instead of living from what has happened. We owe it to God to live aware of what He has done, and draw from the reality He has made available. Not doing so costs us dearly.

The heavens were torn open, and there is no demonic power that is able to sew them back together. Besides, the Father longs for the Spirit who lives in us. What power of darkness exists that could block their fellowship? But when we live with a primary awareness of the enemy and his plans, we instinctively live in reaction to darkness. Again, if I do, then the enemy has had a role in influencing my agenda. And he isn't worthy. My life must be lived in response to what the Father is doing. That is the life Jesus modeled for us.

Heaven is filled with perfect confidence and peace, while this world is filled with chaos and mistrust in God. We always reflect the nature of the world we are most aware of. Living aware of open heavens has incalculable results.[71]

---

71 Hosting the Presence, p. 97-98

THE LATTER
GLORY

The prophets were the most feared because the Spirit of the Lord came upon them. That's it. The Spirit of God, One who, Himself, saturates Heaven with His Presence, rests upon people. And when He does, things happen. These early prophets carried the Presence of God in a way that was rare, especially for their day. Their role is still often misunderstood in ours.

They played a vital role in the increasing revelation of the interaction of God's abiding Presence and the purpose of man on earth. If we can see their history clearly and recognize the momentum created by these great men and women of God, we will be positioned to more readily embrace the assignment for our day. Ours is to be a greater day just as God has promised: "*The latter glory of this house will be greater than the former*" (Haggai 2:9). Plus, we are to have the benefit of greater clarity of heart and mind through advances that previous generations have obtained for us.

So many of these stories give us prophetic glimpses into a coming day—into a day when what was bizarre and odd would become normal. Even now there are things we live with in the church that were once thought rare or impossible. Believe it or not, things are moving forward, progressing.

There is an obvious progression in the revelation of God for His people and an increase in His manifest Presence and glory. He meant it when He said, "*Of the increase of His government and of peace there shall be no end*" (Isaiah 9:7 NKJV). There has only been increase since those words were spoken. We have to adjust how we think and see to not only realize it, but cooperate with what God is doing. Again it says of us, "*But the path of the righteous is like the light of dawn, that shines brighter and brighter until the full day"* (Prov. 4:18). We should and must expect progress.[72]

---

72 Hosting the Presence, p. 66

Who, then, ascends into the presence of the Lord? And who has the privilege of entering into God's Holy Place? Those who are clean— whose works and ways are pure, whose hearts are true and sealed by the truth, those who never deceive, whose words are sure.

(Psalm 24:3-4 TPT)

We can all draw close to him with the veil removed from our faces. And with no veil we all become like mirrors who brightly reflect the glory of the Lord Jesus. We are being transfigured into his very image as we move from one brighter level of glory to another. And this glorious transfiguration comes from the Lord, who is the Spirit.

(2 Corinthians 3:18 TPT)

THE HIGHWAY
OF HOLINESS

There is an environment created in the outpouring of the Spirit in which holiness becomes the normal expression of a people bathed in His presence. Isaiah speaks of this as the *highway of holiness*. A highway is a road designed to expedite travel because obstacles have been removed. It usually involves easy access and has fellow travelers. A highway of holiness allows for a momentum to be created for the people of God to live in purity, effortlessly. It is so significant that even foolish things get covered. This is not to minimize sin or foolishness. It is just to help us to realize that when many live righteously, it creates a momentum where even the weak succeed.

> *A highway shall be there, and a road, And it shall be called the Highway of Holiness. The unclean shall not pass over it, But it shall be for others. Whoever walks the road, although a fool, Shall not go astray.*
>
> (Isaiah 35:8)

This Highway of Holiness will not be known for compromise. There won't be people who outwardly pretend to be holy and inwardly are corrupt. *"Whoever walks the road, although a fool, shall not go astray."* This means that God is creating such a highway in this time of outpouring that it is going to be hard to wander off the road. This concept is difficult for many to embrace, as we are accustomed to the opposite. We have been quick to speak about the "great falling away" but not the great harvest and city transformation that is also a part of end-time prophecy. A day is coming when there will exist a righteous peer pressure, not based on punishment or the fear of man but from His manifested presence: His glory.

I remember being taught that holiness was a list of things we could and could not do—and the "could not do" list was longer than the "could do" list. Mostly what was on the *can do* list was go to church, tithe, give offerings, witness, read your Bible, and pray. Then we'd throw in a potluck now and then, live a good life, and wait for Jesus to come back. But Jesus didn't go through all that He went through so we could be busy with religious activities. As meaningful as those activities can be, they are "unto" something. He placed the Spirit of the resurrected Christ within us that we would conquer something. He is expecting fruit of the impossible from those He has empowered with the same Spirit He was empowered with, all because He is good.[73]

---

73 God is Good, p. 179

CONTAMINATE
WITH
RIGHTEOUSNESS

Without the outpouring of the Spirit, the Church becomes more concerned with being contaminated by evil than we do of "contaminating" the world with righteousness. While we should never take sin lightly, neither should we be ignorant of the power of holiness.

Things are different in the New Testament in that the whole covenant is given to meet the obvious need presented in the Old Testament. For example, the Gospel of Matthew was written primarily for the Jews. In this account of Jesus' life, Jesus touching the leper was the first miracle that

Matthew mentioned as it seemed to help recalibrate the reader's value system to be consistent with the value system of Jesus, Himself. When He touched the leper, the leper became clean. Jesus did what was forbidden to do, bringing about what the Law was unable to do.

This testimony confronted an incomplete mindset that was not adequate for His present work of grace on the earth. The power of holiness becomes even clearer when we read that a believing spouse sanctifies the entire unbelieving household. That is the power of holiness. This Kingdom mindset requires a shift in how we view and value life itself, and the effect of the life of Christ in us. Faith in Kingdom realities manifests Kingdom realities.

The power of holiness becomes clearer in the story of Daniel. God took Daniel and allowed him to be numbered with witches and warlocks before King Nebuchadnezzar. He lived righteously and brought about a New Testament effect of holiness and loyalty on an entire kingdom until that ungodly leader was converted. Holiness is more powerful than sin; it's the purity of Christ in you.[74]

---

74   God is Good, p. 173-174

TWO LEGS

It is true that power is not more important than character. But it is equally true that character is not more important than power. Whenever we make that mistake, the gifts of the Spirit become rewards and are no longer gifts. This emphasis has actually damaged our effectiveness in the gifts of the Spirit. In fact, this approach has caused as much damage in the area of supernatural gifting as flawed character has damaged our witness to the world. Both are essential. Character and power are the two legs we stand on, equal in importance.[75]

---

75 Hosting the Presence, p. 140

John the Baptist saw the dove come upon Jesus and remain. There is no record of anyone else seeing the dove. Yet everyone saw the result of the dove's presence: both in purity and power, displayed to reveal the heart of God for this orphaned planet.

As the Holy Spirit revealed the Father's will to Jesus, so He reveals the Father's heart to us. And His Presence and power reveal the Father through us. Revealing His will is revealing Him.

Jesus became the ultimate revelation of the will of God on earth. But it's not just through what He accomplished. It is through His relentless and consistent hosting of the Dove.

Giving place to the Presence of God as our greatest joy and treasure is not a trick we use to get miracles. But the Father cannot be adequately represented without miracles. They are essential in revealing His nature.

We make the distinction between the natural and the supernatural. Those are the two realms we live in. But God only has one: the natural. It's all natural for Him.[76]

---

76 Hosting the Presence, p. 143-144

HOLINESS
DEMANDS
EXPRESSION

Holiness in character is the manifestation of the power of God touching the nature of man. Holiness also affects the human body with healing. That's why it says, *"The sun of righteousness will rise with healing in its wings"* (Mal. 4:2). Holiness demands expression, and that expression is the manifestation of power. This gives language to what the Spirit of God is doing. The Lord was *"declared to be the Son of God with power according to the Spirit of holiness by the resurrection of the dead"* (Rom. 1:4). Miracles like the resurrection are a normal expression of holiness.

At times our love for God is measured by what we hate. He is still the judge and will always condemn whatever interferes with love. How much did God hate sickness? As much as He hated sin. They are dealt with almost as one and the same. What sin is to my soul, sickness is to my body. He hated sickness enough to allow His Son to experience such a brutal beating. The blood covers our sin, but the wounds paid for our healing. That is how much He hates sin AND sickness. We cannot be tolerant of those things, because what we tolerate dominates.[77]

---

77 God is Good, p. 181-182

And when they had prayed, the place where they had gathered together was shaken, and they were all filled with the Holy Spirit and began to speak the word of God with boldness.

(Acts 4:31 NASB)

He said to them, "It is not for you to know times or epochs which the Father has fixed by His own authority; but you will receive power when the Holy Spirit has come upon you; and you shall be My witnesses both in Jerusalem, and in all Judea and Samaria, and even to the remotest part of the earth."

(Acts 1:7-8 NASB)

RELEASE
OF POWER

Picture this well-known story in Jesus' life: The streets are crowded with people who are hungry for more. Some are in pursuit of God; others just want to be close to this man who has become so famous for wonderful things. He has raised the dead, healed the sick, and has become the single subject of a whole town. People followed Jesus anywhere and everywhere. As this throng of people are walking down the road, a woman, a very desperate woman, sees her chance for a miracle. She has carried her affliction for many years without any hope of recovery. She presses into the crowd until Jesus is within reach. But she is way too embarrassed to talk to Him or even get His attention. She merely reaches out to touch the edge of His clothing.

> *Now a woman, having a flow of blood for twelve years, who had spent all her livelihood on physicians and could not be healed by any, came from behind and touched the border of His garment. And immediately her flow of blood stopped. And Jesus said, "Who touched Me?" When all denied it, Peter and those with him said, "Master, the multitudes throng and press You, and You say, 'Who touched Me?'" But Jesus said, "Somebody touched Me, for I perceived power going out from Me."*

(Luke 8:43-45)

It's important to understand at the beginning of this story that power in the Kingdom of God is in the form of a person. It is not a separate entity apart from God Himself. Jesus realized that anointing, the person of the Holy Spirit, was released from

Him by the demand of somebody else's faith. This really is amazing.

Now it's one thing to become aware of the Presence of God in worship, and quite another to realize when the Holy Spirit is released from us in ministry. On occasion, I have felt the anointing of the Holy Spirit released from my hands when I've prayed for someone for healing. It's so encouraging. But it is a whole new level to be so aware of the Holy Spirit who rests upon us that we notice when someone else's faith has put a demand on what we carry. It can be said that she made a withdrawal from Jesus' account. How aware of the person of the Holy Spirit do we have to be to notice such a release of power when it flows from us? Add to this equation that Jesus was walking and talking with others when this happened. To me, this is astonishing. He is conscious of the Presence even when He is talking to others or listening to their comments and questions. It is for this that I am most jealous.

A withdrawal was made from the One who has been given the Spirit without measure. An anointing cannot be depleted. It wasn't the lack of anointing He discovered. It was the Holy Spirit moving that He recognized—the Holy Spirit was released from Him. This amazes me beyond words.[78]

---

78 Hosting the Presence, p. 135

KATHRYN
KUHLMAN

One of those I admire most is Kathryn Kuhlman. I actually had the privilege to see her on several occasions as a young man. I respect her so much, for so many reasons. The miracles that came forth in her meetings are certainly one of the reasons. But let's lay that aside for a moment. Without being disrespectful, I'd like to tell you what she wasn't.

She wasn't known as a great Bible teacher, or a great preacher, although she could do both. She didn't have natural beauty that seems to exalt others to a place of favor with man ahead of their appointed time. She wasn't a great singer, moving crowds with an amazing voice. And the list goes on. What could she do? She just seemed to be the person that God liked to be with. She is known for the Presence. The miracles came from that one thing. The mass conversions came from that one thing. The high places of worship that were experienced in her meetings came from that one thing. She was a Presence woman.

I still get teary-eyed when I watch the video where she talks about her point of absolute surrender to the Holy Spirit. It is a sobering moment indeed. She testifies of the precise moment, the precise location where she said the ultimate yes to God. Those moments don't reveal our strength. They actually reveal our weaknesses. To be all we can be requires that we are more dependent on God.[79]

---

79 Hosting the Presence, p. 61

LIVING
BEYOND REASON

Following the anointing (the Holy Spirit) is very similar to Israel following the cloud of the Lord's presence in the wilderness. The Israelites had no control over Him. He led, and the people followed. Wherever He went, supernatural activities took place. If they departed from the cloud, the miracles that sustained them would be gone. Can you imagine what would have happened if our fear-oriented theologians had been there? They would have created new doctrines explaining why the supernatural ministry that brought them out of Egypt was no longer necessary to bring them into the Promised Land. After all, now they had the tablets of stone. Then, as today, the real issue is the priority we place upon His presence. When that's intact, the supernatural abounds, but without it we have to make up new doctrines for why we're OK as we are.

In New Testament terms, being a people focused on His presence means that we are willing to live beyond reason. Not impulsively or foolishly, for these are poor imitations for real faith. The realm beyond reason is the world of obedience to God. Obedience is the expression of faith, and faith is our claim ticket to the God realm. Strangely, this focus on His presence causes us to become like wind, which is also the nature of the Holy Spirit (see John 3:8). His nature is powerful and righteous, but His ways cannot be controlled. He is unpredictable.

As church leaders, this hits us at our weakest point. For most churches, very little of what we do is dependent upon the Holy Spirit. If He were not to show up, most churches would never miss Him. Billy Graham is credited with saying, "Ninety-five percent of today's church activities would continue if the Holy Spirit were removed from us. In the early Church, ninety-five percent of all her activities would have stopped if the Holy Spirit were removed." I agree.

We plan our services, and call it diligence. We plan our year, and call it vision. I'll never forget the Sunday that the Lord informed me that it wasn't my service, and I couldn't do as I pleased. (Planning is biblical. But our diligence and vision must never include usurping the authority of the Holy Spirit. The Lordship of Jesus is seen in our willingness to follow the Holy Spirit's leading. He wants His Church back!) But how can we follow Him if we don't recognize His presence?

The more pronounced His presence, the more unique the manifestations of our God encounters become. Although the manifestations we experience while encountering Him are important, it's God Himself we long for.[80]

---

80 When Heaven Invades Earth, p. 90-91

GREEN
LIGHT

Many believers live with the concept that God will lead them when it's time for them to do something. And so they wait, sometimes for an entire lifetime, without any significant impact on the world around them. Their philosophy—I have a red light until God gives me a green one. The green light never comes.

The apostle Paul lived in the *green light district* of the gospel. He didn't need signs in the heavens to convince him to obey the Scriptures. When Jesus said, "Go!" that was enough. But He still needed the Holy Spirit to show him what was at the forefront of the Father's mind concerning missions.

He had a burden for Asia, and tried to go there and preach. The Holy Spirit stopped him, which also means He didn't lead him. He then tried to go to Bithynia, but again, the Holy Spirit said no. He then had a dream of a man pleading with him to come to Macedonia. He woke up concluding that this was the direction he was looking for, and went to Macedonia to preach the gospel. It's a wonderful story of God's leading (see Acts 16:6-10).

But it's easy to miss the point; Paul was trying to obey what was on the pages of Scripture because he lived carrying the commandment *to go into all the world!* (see Matt. 28:19). The old adage comes into play here; it's easier to steer the car when it's moving than when it's standing still. Paul's commitment to the lifestyle of *going* put him in the place to hear the specific directions God had for him in that season. It was the Holy Spirit who was trying to keep him from going to certain places in wrong seasons.[81]

---

81 Dreaming with God, p. 129-130

Those who are motivated by the flesh only pursue what benefits themselves. But those who live by the impulses of the Holy Spirit are motivated to pursue spiritual realities. For the mind-set of the flesh is death, but the mind-set controlled by the Spirit finds life and peace.

(Romans 8:5-6 TPT)

THE DOVE
THAT REMAINS

The world thinks of peace as the absence of something: a time without war, a time without noise, or a time without conflict. For a believer, Peace is a person—the presence of someone. Our ability to respond to this command of Jesus to release peace over a household is central in His instruction for ministry. It is tied directly to our ability to recognize the Presence of the Holy Spirit. It's hard to release with any consistency what you're not aware of. Consciousness of Presence will always increase our impact when it comes to influencing the world around us.

So much of what we do is done out of ministry principles instead of out of the Presence. One of the mysteries of life is that a primary role of a believer is the stewardship of a person, the Abiding Presence, who is the Holy Spirit—the dove that remains. He is a person, not an it. When we reduce the joy of knowing God to the principles that bring break-through, we cheapen the journey. Those who desire principles above Presence seek a kingdom without a king.

Jesus is called the Prince of Peace in Scripture. The Holy Spirit is the Spirit of Christ, the person of peace. And that Peace that is a person is the actual atmosphere of Heaven. That is why peace is like a double-edged sword: it is calming and wonderful for the believer, but highly destructive and invasive for the powers of darkness. *"The God of peace will soon crush Satan under your feet"* (Romans 16:20). That's quite an assignment given to His followers: release the person of peace when you enter a home, for in doing so, you will release the Presence that is the actual atmosphere of Heaven to yielded hearts while at the same time undermining the powers of darkness that are at work in that home. For that atmosphere is expressed through the person of the Holy Spirit. For Jesus, this was Ministry 101.[82]

---

82   Hosting the Presence, p. 149-150

SENDING OUT
THE DOVE

A rather surprising place in Scripture to find Jesus' lesson for His disciples is in the story of Noah and the flood. There's one part of the story that illustrates in an Old Testament context what Jesus would train His disciples to do.

So it came to pass, at the end of forty days, that Noah opened the window of the ark which he had made. Then he sent out a raven, which kept going to and fro until the waters had dried up from the earth. He also sent out from himself a dove, to see if the waters had receded from the face of the ground. But the dove found no resting place for the sole of her foot, and she returned into the ark to him, for the waters were on the face of the whole earth. So he put out his hand and took her, and drew her into the ark to himself.

(Genesis 8:6-9)

I remind you that the dove represents the Holy Spirit in Scripture. This is especially clear in the story of Jesus' water baptism. And here in the story of Noah we find an interesting description of Noah's connection with the dove. There is no other animal that received the same attention or had the implied bond with Noah as did this dove.

The dove was released because he would look for a resting place. When he didn't find a place to rest, he returned to Noah and the ark. That is the picture given of the release of the Holy Spirit through the disciples as they go into someone's home. The implication is that the Holy Spirit is still looking for places to rest—and those places are people. When the dove couldn't find a place to rest, he returned to Noah, the sender. Once again consider Jesus' words concerning their release of peace to a home. If there's no one there that will host this Presence well, *"it will return to you"* (Luke 10:6). When the dove could find no place to rest, the dove came back. Noah put out his hand and brought the dove back to himself. It is interesting phrasing: "from himself" and "to himself." This is an Old Testament glimpse into New Testament ministry...

The [third] time he released the dove it didn't return. I believe for most of us this lesson is abstract because we receive so little teaching and experience in learning to recognize the Presence of God. Most would never know in a ministry situation if the dove was released, or better yet if He came back. It would be really tough to know if the Holy Spirit that was released from us is now resting upon someone. I state this not to shame anyone but to create hunger for what is legally our privilege and responsibility. We are to know the ways and Presence of the Holy Spirit so we can cooperate with Him in a way that changes the world around us. This is true ministry.[83]

---

83   Hosting the Presence, p.152-153

JUSTICE
MUST PREVAIL

Buck was a man who fully embraced taking the gifts into the market place. He was selected for jury duty. As soon as he sat down, the Lord spoke to him: "Justice must prevail." When the trial phase was finally over and the jury began to deliberate, they found themselves divided as to the interpretation of the law. Buck explained the issues in such a remarkable way that the others thought he had studied law. He used that opportunity to share his testimony. He was once a great science student, but his mind had been ravished by a lifestyle of drug addiction. Jesus healed his mind as he memorized Scripture. His testimony won the hearts of some jurists, but drove others away.

When it was time to cast their verdict, they were evenly divided. So the deliberations carried over to the next day. Their point of contention was the definition of a *criminal*. The man being tried fit six of the seven qualifications needed for him to be considered guilty. The seventh was questionable. So Buck brought a rose in a vase the next day of deliberations. Everyone thought it was a nice gesture. He let them argue for a while and then asked them, "What is this on the table?" They looked at him like he was stupid, and said, "A rose!" He asked them if they were sure, and they said yes.

He pressed them further asking, "What are the parts that make up a rose?" They listed the petals, stem, leaves, thorns, etc. So he asked them, "Do you see all those parts of this rose?" They responded, "Yes, everything but the thorns." So he asked, "Is it still a rose without those thorns?" They said, "Yes!" To which he stated, "And this man is a criminal!"

They got the message. The gift of wisdom had been in operation without their knowing it. Now all but two agreed he was guilty. It was still a hung jury.

When the judge asked each juror if they believed they could come to an agreement, they all said no. That is, except Buck. In His heart were the words, *"justice must prevail."* The judge then gave them 30 minutes to work through their disagreement. As soon as they entered the room for deliberation, the word of the Lord came to Buck. He pointed to one of the two jurors and said, "You say he's innocent because..." Buck proceeded to expose a secret sin in the juror's life. He then turned to the other and did the same. They both looked at each other and said, "I'll change my vote if you change yours!"

Buck first brought the gift of wisdom into the deliberations. It helped to bring clarification that benefited even unbelievers. He then brought a word of knowledge, something that he could not have known in the natural, to expose the sin in two people who had rejected God's dealings. In the end, the will of God prevailed in the situation—*justice!*

Being involved in the supernatural through spiritual gifts is what makes the invasion effective. The Kingdom of God is a Kingdom of power! We must be in pursuit of a fuller demonstration of the Spirit of God. Pray much and take risks.[84]

---

84 When Heaven Invades Earth, p. 199-201

Thy kingdom come, Thy will be done in earth, as it is in heaven.

(Matthew 6:10 KJV)

SALT
AND LIGHT

Part of the privilege of ministry is learning how to release the Holy Spirit in a location. When I pastored in Weaverville, California, our church offices were downtown, located directly across from one bar and right next to another. This downtown area was the commercial center for the entire county—a perfect place for a church office!

It's not good when Christians try to do business only with other Christians. We are salt and light. We shine best in dark places! I love business and business people and have genuine interest in their success. Before entering a store, I often pray for the Holy Spirit to be released through me. If I need something on one side of the store, I'll enter on the opposite end in order to walk through the entire store. Many opportunities for ministry have developed as I've learned how to release His presence in the marketplace.

People laid the sick in the streets hoping that Peter's shadow would fall on them and they'd be healed (see Acts 5:15). Nevertheless, it wasn't Peter's shadow that brought healing. There is no substance to a shadow. Peter was *overshadowed* by the Holy Spirit, and it was that presence that brought the miracles. The anointing is an expression of the person of the Holy Spirit. He is tangible. There were times in Jesus' ministry when everyone who touched Christ's clothing was healed or delivered (see Mark 6:56). The anointing is substance. It is the actual presence of the Holy Spirit, and He can be released into our surroundings.[85]

---

85   When Heaven Invades Earth, p. 83-84

RELEASING
THE PRESENCE

Jesus explained an especially important part of the Christian life of ministry when He said, *"The words that I have spoken to you are spirit and are life"* (John 6:63). Jesus is the word made flesh. But when He spoke, the word became Spirit. That is what happens whenever we say what the Father is saying. We've all experienced this: we are in a troubling situation, and someone walks in the room and says something that changes the atmosphere of the entire room. It wasn't merely because they came in with a great idea. They spoke something that became material—a substance that changed the atmosphere. What happened? They spoke something timely and purposeful. They said what the Father was saying. Words become spirit.

Words are the tools with which God created the world. The spoken word is also central to creating faith in us (see Romans 10:17). His spoken word is creative in nature. Saying what the Father is saying releases the creative nature and Presence of God into a situation to bring His influence and change.[86]

---

86   Hosting the Presence, p.163-164

RELEASING
THE PRESENCE:
ACTS OF FAITH

His Presence accompanies His acts. Faith brings a substantial release of Presence, which is visible time after time in Jesus' ministry. An act of faith is any action on the outside that demonstrates the faith on the inside. For example, I've told people to run on a severely injured ankle or leg. As soon as they do, they are healed. How? The Presence is released in the action.

That is something I would never do out of the principle of faith. I am only willing to give that direction out of the Presence. Many leaders make a huge mistake at this point. I will never require someone to put themselves at risk out of a principle. If I am experiencing what appears to be a roadblock in my walk with Christ, I will at times require a bold act of myself out of principle—but never someone else.[87]

---

87   Hosting the Presence, p. 164

RELEASING
THE PRESENCE:
PROPHETIC ACT

A Prophetic Act is a unique facet of the Christian life as it requires an action that by appearance has no connection to the desired outcome. Whereas stepping on an injured ankle is connected to the desired outcome—a healed ankle—a prophetic act has no connection. A great example would be when Elisha was told about a borrowed axe head that fell into the river. It says, *"He cut off a stick and threw it in there, and made the iron float"* (2 Kings 6:6). You can throw sticks in the water all day long and never make an axe head swim. The act is seemingly unrelated. The strength of the prophetic act is that it comes from the heart of the Father. It is a prophetic act of obedience that has a logic outside human reasoning.

I've seen this happen many times when someone is wanting a miracle. I've had them move from where they were sitting and stand in the aisle of the church. It wasn't because there was more power of the Holy Spirit in the aisle. It's because it was a prophetic act that would release the presence of the Holy Spirit upon them. Jesus operated in this many times. He once told a blind man to wash in the pool of Siloam (see John 9:7). There is no healing power in the pool. The miracle was released in the act of going and washing—both logically unrelated to the desired outcome.[88]

---

88   Hosting the Presence, p. 164-165

RELEASING THE PRESENCE: TOUCH

The laying on of hands is one of the primary doctrines of the church specifically referred to as a doctrine of Christ (see Hebrews 6:1-2). It was a practice in the Old Testament, too. The priest laid his hands on a goat to symbolically release the sins of Israel on that goat that would then be released into the wilderness. The laying on of hands upon the goat was to release something that would help Israel come into their purpose. It was also used to impart authority, as in the case of Moses and his elders. The apostle Paul laid his hands on Timothy to release apostolic commissioning. In Acts, hands were laid on people for the release of the Holy Spirit upon them (see Acts 8:18). The point is this: laying hands on people to release something of God into people's lives. It is a tool that God uses to release the reality of His world, His Presence, upon another.[89]

---

89 Hosting the Presence, p.165

RELEASING
THE PRESENCE:
WORSHIP

Worship has an unusual effect on our surroundings. We know that He inhabits our praise (see Ps. 22:3). It stands to reason that Presence is released. Atmosphere is changed. In fact, the atmosphere of Jerusalem came about in part because of worship. *"We hear them in our own tongues speaking of the mighty deeds of God"* (Acts 2:11). Such praise contributed to an atmospheric shift over an entire city where the spiritual blindness was lifted, followed by 3,000 souls being saved.

I've seen this myself when we've rented a particular facility for church services, only to have the people who use it afterward comment on the Presence that remains. A friend of mine used to take people onto the streets in San Francisco many years ago. They met with heavy resistance. But when he realized that when God arises, His enemies are scattered, he strategically used this approach for ministry (see Ps. 68). He split his team into two. One half went out to worship, and the other half would minister to people. The police then came to him and told him that when he is on the streets, crime stops. This is an amazing result from a dove being released over a part of the city. The atmosphere changes as the Presence is given His rightful place.[90]

---

90 Hosting the Presence, p. 166-167

YOUR
KINGDOM COME

When we pray for His Kingdom to come, we are asking Him to superimpose the rules, order, and benefits of His world over this one until this one looks like His. That's what happens when the sick are healed or the demonized are set free. His world collides with the world of darkness, and His world always wins. Our battle is always a battle for dominion—a conflict of kingdoms.[91]

---

91 When Heaven Invades Earth, p. 71

We have been given authority over this planet. It was first given to us in the commission God gave to mankind in Genesis (see Gen. 1:28-29), and was then restored to us by Jesus after His resurrection (see Matt. 28:18). But kingdom authority is different than is typically understood by many believers. It is the authority to set people free from torment and disease, destroying the works of darkness. It is the authority to move the resources of Heaven through creative expression to meet human need. It is the authority to bring Heaven to earth. It is the authority to serve.

As with most kingdom principles, the truths of mankind's dominion and authority are dangerous in the hands of those who desire to rule over others. These concepts seem to validate some people's selfishness. But when these truths are expressed through the humble servant, the world is rocked to its core. Becoming servants to this world is the key to open the doors of possibility that are generally thought of as closed or forbidden.

Neither our understanding of servants or of kings can help us much with this challenge for both are soiled in our world, probably beyond repair. That is where Jesus comes in. He is the King of all kings, yet the Servant of all. This unique combination found in the Son of God is the call of the hour upon us. As truth is usually found in the tension of two conflicting realities, we have an issue to solve. Like our Master, we are both royalty and servants (see Rev. 1:5).

Solomon warns of a potential problem, saying, *"the earth cannot bear up under a slave when he becomes king"* (Prov. 30:21-22). Yet Jesus contradicted Solomon's warning without nullifying the statement, by being effective at both. *Jesus served with the heart of a king, but ruled with the heart of a servant.* This is the essential combination that must be embraced by those longing to shape the course of history.

Royalty is my identity. Servanthood is my assignment. Intimacy with God is my life source. So, before God, I'm an intimate. Before man, I'm a servant. Before the powers of hell, I'm a ruler, with no tolerance for their influence. Wisdom knows which role to fulfill at the proper time.[92]

---

92 Dreaming with God, p. 87-88

POWER
ENCOUNTER

uthority comes with the commission, but power comes with the encounter. They were commanded not to leave until they had their encounter with the Spirit of God. In Matthew 28, they received authority, but in Acts 2, they received power. To this day this is true: authority comes from the commission, and power comes from the encounter. And while these two elements seem to have their primary focus on ministry, they are first the essential elements for our engaging the Holy Spirit for relationship. Power and authority introduce us to the nature of the Holy Spirit with a primary focus on hosting His Presence. Ministry should flow out of the relationship with the person who lives in us for our sakes, but rests upon us for the sake of others.[93]

Power brings breakthrough. Miracles happen often because of the power of God released in and through His people. Wherever we see the power of God displayed, we see transformation and change. Miracles, signs, and wonders are the fruit of the Holy Spirit's power in the life of the believing believer.

Power is the purpose behind the baptism of the Holy Spirit: *"But you shall receive power..."* (Acts 1:8). Yet the second manifestation of power is equally important. It is the ability to endure until the answer comes. There are two sides to this coin— breakthrough and endurance. It is the exact same concept that we saw with faith. We must develop

---

93 Hosting the Presence, p. 162

the lifestyle of endurance without embracing the lack of breakthrough as the norm.[94]

---

94 God is Good, p. 226-227

And Jesus came and spoke to them, saying, "All authority has been given to Me in heaven and on earth. Go therefore and make disciples of all the nations, baptizing them in the name of the Father and of the Son and of the Holy Spirit, teaching them to observe all things that I have commanded you; and lo, I am with you always, even to the end of the age."

(Matthew 28:18-20 NKJV)

FRIENDS OF GOD

This unimaginable privilege of carrying His presence should never reduce me to a laborer for God. The decision of being a servant or a friend is still being chosen by people around us every day. While it is one of my highest privileges to serve Him completely, my labor is the byproduct of my love. This baptism introduces us to intimacy at the highest possible level. The heart of God in this matter is clearly seen in this amazing prophecy from Ezekiel. "*I will not hide **my face** from them anymore, for I shall have poured out **my Spirit***" (Ezekiel 39:29). In the outpouring of the Holy Spirit is the revelation of the face of God. There is nothing greater.[95]

---

95 Hosting the Presence, p. 109-110

No longer do I call you servants, for a servant does not know what his master is doing; but I have called you friends, for all things that I heard from My Father I have made known to you.

(John 15:15)

With this promotion, the disciples' attention would now shift from the task at hand to the One within reach. They were given access to the secrets in the heart of God.

When Jesus gave His disciples this promotion, He did so by describing the difference between the two positions. Servants don't know what their master is doing. They don't have access to the personal, intimate realm of their master. They are task-oriented. Obedience is their primary focus – and rightly so, for their lives depend on success in that area. But friends have a different focus. It almost sounds blasphemous to say that obedience is not the top concern for the friend, but it is true. Obedience will always be important, as the previous verse highlights, *"You are my friends if you do whatever I command you"* (John 15:14). But friends are less concerned about disobeying than they are about disappointing. The disciples' focus shifted from the commandments to the presence, from the assignment to the relationship, from "what I do for Him" to "how my choices affect Him." This bestowal of friendship made the revolution we continue to experience possible.[96]

---

96 Dreaming with God, p. 24

CO-CREATORS
WITH GOD

Here is the picture: The Presence of God is hosted by a person so significantly that He actually lives through them. It's not cancelling out who they are. It's capturing it to the fullest, immersed in divine influence. It is as though their personality, their gifts and demeanor are all being expressed through God living in them.[97]

God created us with desires and passions, and the capacity to dream. All of these traits are necessary

97 Hosting the Presence, p. 79

to truly make us like Him. With these abilities, we can discover more of God, our purpose in life, and the beauty and fullness of His kingdom. When these abilities exist unharnessed by divine purpose, they take us to forbidden fruit. It was a risk God was willing to take in order to end up with His dream—those made in His image, who worship Him by choice, who carry His Presence into all the earth.[98]

The King James Bible highlights the role of our desires in the way it translates Mark 11:24, *"Therefore I say unto you, what things soever ye desire, when ye pray, believe that ye receive them, and ye shall have them."* We are to pay attention to our desires *while we're enjoying the presence of God in prayer.* Something happens in our time of communion with Him that brings life to our capacity to dream and desire. Our minds become renewed through divine encounter, making it the perfect canvas for Him to

98   Hosting the Presence, p. 93-94

paint on. We become co-laborers with Him in the master plan for planet earth.

Our dreams are not independent from God, but instead exist *because of* God. He lays out the agenda – *On earth as it is in Heaven* – and then releases us to run with it and make it happen! As we grow in intimacy with Him, more of what happens in life is a result of our desires, not simply receiving and obeying specific commands from Heaven. God loves to build on our wishes and desires, as He embraced David's desire for the temple.

This truth is risky from our perspective because we see those who live independent of God and only want Him to validate their dreams. True grace always creates a place for those with evil in their heart to come to the surface through increased opportunity. But the richness of this truth is worth pursuing in spite of the perceived danger, because only this truth enables the church to come fully into her destiny through co-laboring with the Lord.

This divine destiny was announced by the Psalmist long before the blood of Jesus made it a possible lifestyle. *"Delight yourself also in the LORD, and He shall give you the desires of your heart"* (Psalms 37:4).[99]

---

99 Dreaming with God, p. 34-35

CREATIVE CONVERSATION

Time in His Presence will release creative ideas. When I spend time with God, I remember phone calls I need to make, projects I long forgot about, and things I had planned to do with my wife or my children. Ideas flow freely in this environment because that's the way He is. I get ideas in the Presence I wouldn't get anywhere else. Insights on how to fix problems or people that need to be affirmed all come in that exchange of fellowship between God and man.

We must stop blaming the devil for all those interruptions. (Many of us have too big a devil and too small a God.) And while the enemy of our souls will work to distract us from the Presence, he's often blamed when he is nowhere near because we misunderstand our Father and what He values.

When we realize that often it's God interacting with us, we are able to enjoy the process much more and give Him thanks for having concern for these parts of our lives that we might often think are too small for His input. If it matters to you, it matters to Him. These ideas are the fruit of our two-way conversation. But in order to keep from leaving the privilege of interaction with God to work on other things, I write these things down so I can return to my worship and fellowship with Him. The notes I write are to give me directions I can return to later.

Because God is resting upon us, we should expect new levels of creative ideas with which to impact our world. By referring to creative, I'm not just talking about painting or writing songs, etc. Creativity is the touch of the Creator on every part of life. It's the need of the accountant and the lawyer as much as it is for the musician and actor. It is to be expected when you're the son or daughter of the Creator, Himself.[100]

---

100 Hosting the Presence, p. 175-176

GIVING UP
CONTROL

It would be foolish to think the danger of front-lines kind of ministry isn't real. But when the manifest presence of God is with you in your assignment, dangerous places become safe. And the measure we are aware of our need for Him is usually the measure we become aware of Him. It really is all about the Presence. It's about hosting Him. This is what the 70 discovered. Neither their ignorance nor lack of experience disqualified them. They had been sent by One who was going with them (see Luke 10).

I would have provided all the natural things they needed. Jesus provided the direction and the Presence as seen in the power and authority given to them. What He gave them insures the natural provisions will be there because the Holy Spirit is at work. This is the concept that Jesus taught the multitudes in Matt 6:33, *"Seek first the kingdom of God...and all these things will be added."* His Kingdom works entirely on the first things first principle. The provision of the Lord is not just food on the table. The supernatural provision of the Lord is divine protection and full impact in our assignment. That is the whole issue: Giving up the reins of being in control of my life to become truly Holy Spirit empowered and directed. His commission was to go learn how the Holy Spirit moves. Go learn His ways.[101]

Trust in the Lord with all your heart and do not lean on your own understanding. *In all your ways acknowledge Him, and He will make your paths straight.* (Prov. 3:5-6)

---

101 Hosting the Presence, p. 152

Trust will take us beyond understanding into realms that only faith can discover. Trust is built on interaction, and the resulting discovery of His nature, which is good and perfect in every way. We don't believe because we understand. We understand because we believe. Understanding that comes this way is the renewed mind. Discovering a fuller expression of God's nature and Presence is exponentially increased with this simple element called trust.

To acknowledge Him is what we do when we trust Him. The one we trust above our own existence is to be recognized in every aspect and part of life. The word 'acknowledge' actually means to know. It is an unusually big word in Scripture, with a broad range of meanings. But the one thing that stands out to me the most is that this word often points to the realm of personal experience. It is bigger than head knowledge. It is beyond concepts alone. It is a knowing through encounter. In fact, Genesis 4:1 it says, "*And Adam knew Eve his wife; and she conceived, and bare Cain*" (KJV). Obviously, a word of this nature is more than an idea. It is deep interaction.[102]

---

102 Hosting the Presence, p. 171

ALL FLESH

And it shall come to pass in the last days, says God, That I will pour out of My Spirit on all flesh; Your sons and your daughters shall prophesy, Your young men shall see visions, Your old men shall dream dreams. And on My menservants and on My maidservants I will pour out My Spirit in those days; And they shall prophesy.

(Acts 2:17-21)

This passage quoted from Joel 2 has never been completely fulfilled. It had initial fulfillment in Acts 2, but its reach was far greater than that generation could fulfill. First of all, *all flesh* was never touched by that revival. But it will happen. In the coming move of God, racial barriers will be broken, as will the economic, sexual, and age barriers. The outpouring of the Spirit in the last generation will touch every nation on the earth, releasing the gifts of the Spirit in full measure upon and through His people.

First Corinthians 12-14 is a wonderful teaching on the operation of the gifts of the Spirit. But it is so much more. It is a revelation of a body of believers who live in the realm of the Spirit that is essential for last days' ministry. These manifestations of the Holy Spirit will be taken to the streets where they belong. It is there that they reach their full potential.

This generation will fulfill the cry of Moses for all of God's people to be prophets. We will carry the Elijah anointing in preparing for the return of the Lord in the same way that John the Baptist carried the Elijah anointing and prepared the people for the coming of the Lord.[103]

---

103 When Heaven Invades Earth, p. 212

We are the ones upon whom the promises of the ages have come to rest. And they are contingent upon our being a people who have discovered our eternal purpose. We have been chosen to be His eternal dwelling place. We have been chosen to host His Presence.[104]

104 Hosting the Presence, p. 203

ABOUT BILL
JOHNSON

BILL JOHNSON is a fifth-generation pastor with a rich heritage in the Holy Spirit. Bill and his wife, Beni, are the senior leaders of Bethel Church in Redding, California, and serve a growing number of churches that cross denominational lines, demonstrate power, and partner for revival. Bill's vision is for all believers to experience God's presence and operate in the miraculous—as expressed in his bestselling books *When Heaven Invades Earth* and *Hosting the Presence*. The Johnsons have three children and ten grandchildren.

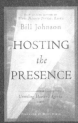